THE STUDY SCHOOL
NEW MALDEN

Teacher's Resource Book 4

Barry and Anita Scholes

Authors: Barry and Anita Scholes

Design: Grasshopper Design Company; Amanda Easter

Editor: Janet Swarbrick

Cover image: Renee Lynn, Tony Stone Images

Illustrations: Pat Murray

Published by Collins Educational
An imprint of HarperCollins*Publishers* Ltd
77–85 Fulham Palace Road
Hammersmith
London W6 8JB

Browse the complete Collins catalogue at
www.collinseducation.com

www.harpercollins.co.uk
Visit the book lover's website

First published 1999

16 15 14 13

Text © Barry and Anita Scholes 1999
Design and illustrations © HarperCollins*Publishers* Ltd 1999

Barry and Anita Scholes assert the moral right to be identified as the authors of this work.

All rights reserved. Any educational institution that has purchased one copy of this book may make duplicate copies of pages identified as copiable for use exclusively within that institution. (Copiable pages can be identified by the copyright notice printed at the bottom of the page.) No other part of this publication may be reproduced, stored in a retrieval system or transmitted in any form or by any means – electronic, mechanical, photocopying, recording or otherwise – without either the prior written permission of the Publisher or a licence permitting restricted copying in the United Kingdom issued by the Copyright Licensing Agency Ltd, 90 Tottenham Court Road, London W1P 0LP.

ISBN-13 978-0-00-302520-0
ISBN-10 0-00-302520-9

British Library Cataloguing in Publication Data
A catalogue record for this book is available from the British Library.

Printed in Great Britain by Martins the Printers, Berwick-upon-Tweed

Contents

Focus on Literacy and the National Literacy Strategy

You will find in *Focus on Literacy* a strong support in the teaching of reading and writing within the context of a literacy hour. All the literacy objectives of the National Literary Strategy for each term may be covered by using the big book anthologies together with the pupil's book, the homework book, the copymasters and the teacher's resource book. Here, in one grand design, are sufficient teaching materials for five full literacy hours per week throughout the entire school year.

The aims of *Focus on Literacy*

The aims of *Focus on Literacy* are identical to those of the National Literacy Strategy: to develop each child's ability to read and write. It promotes their development by honing the literary skills necessary to meet the Range, Key Skills, and Standard English and Language Study of the National Curriculum Programmes of Study.

These skills are wide-ranging and specific, and worthy of review:

- to read and write with confidence, fluency and understanding
- to use a full range of reading cues (phonic, graphic, syntactic, contextual) to self-monitor their reading and correct their own mistakes
- to understand the sound and spelling system and use this to read and spell accurately
- to acquire fluent and legible handwriting
- to have an interest in words and word meanings, and to increase vocabulary
- to know, understand and be able to write in a range of genres in fiction and poetry, and understand and be familiar with some of the ways that narratives are structured through basic literary ideas of setting, character and plot
- to understand and be able to use a range of non-fiction texts
- to plan, draft, revise and edit their own writing
- to have a suitable technical vocabulary through which to understand and discuss their reading and writing
- to be interested in books, read with enjoyment and evaluate and justify preferences
- to develop their powers of imagination, inventiveness and critical awareness through reading and writing.

The NLS framework and *Focus on Literacy*

The NLS teaching objectives for reading and writing are set out in termly units to ensure progression. Each term's work focuses on specific reading genres and related writing activities. *Focus on Literacy* offers carefully selected examples of these reading genres and stimulating activities relating to them.

The overall structure is the same for each term and is divided into three strands: text, sentence and word levels. Text level refers to comprehension and composition, sentence level to grammar and punctuation and word level to phonics, spelling and vocabulary. The activities in *Focus on Literacy* offer many opportunities for the development of handwriting, while leaving you free to follow your school's own writing policy.

The Literacy Hour and *Focus on Literacy*

The NLS framework requires a literacy hour as part of school work each day. The literacy hour is designed to establish a common pattern for all classes and is carefully structured to ensure a balance between whole class and group teaching, as the diagram below shows.

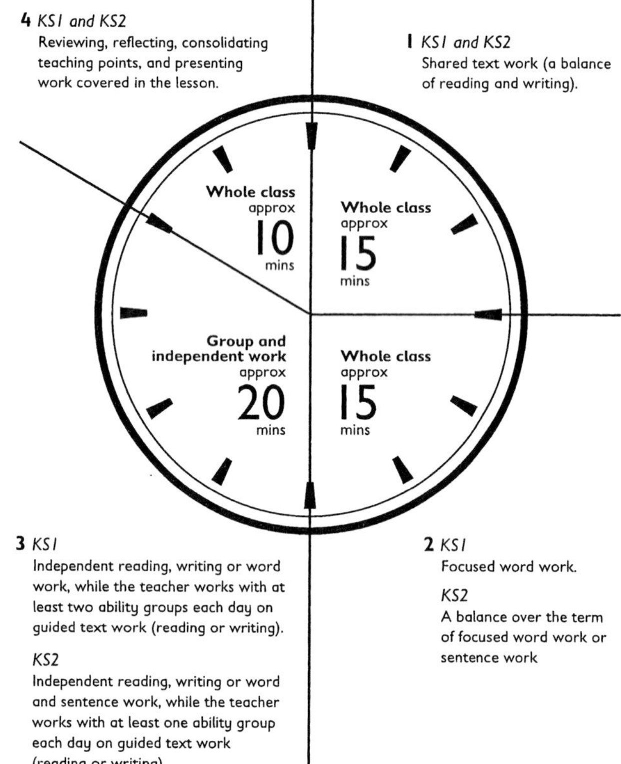

This structure enables you to spend up to 100 per cent of your time in direct teaching. Children work in a direct teaching relationship for approximately 60 per cent of the time and independently for the remaining 40 per cent.

The high quality texts of ***Focus on Literacy*** and the related activities directly meet the NLS objectives, and so relieve you of the burden of deciding *what* to teach. The teacher's notes support you in planning *how* to use the materials in your teaching.

Shared whole class time

Shared whole class time takes place during the first half of the literacy hour. It is divided into 15 minutes of shared text work (a balance of reading and writing) and 15 minutes of focused word and sentence work. This is the time when you can effectively model the reading/writing process with the children.

In shared reading you can help to extend reading skills in line with the NLS objectives, teaching and reinforcing grammar, punctuation and vocabulary.

The reading texts also provide ideas and structures for shared writing. Working with the whole class, you create the opportunity to teach grammar and spelling skills, to demonstrate features of layout and presentation and to focus on editing and refining work. The shared writing will also be the starting point for independent writing.

Independent activities

The shared whole class time of the literacy hour is followed by 20 minutes of independent activities. During this time you will probably work with a guided reading or writing group, while the children will be working independently, but within a group organised by ability to cater for differentiation.

To help you with this, the word and sentence work in the pupil's book is divided into two, three or four sections identified as A, B, C and D; A is the easiest and D is the hardest. It is important to match carefully these activities to the children's ability, and to explain them thoroughly before the children begin. This leaves you free to work with your group without interruptions seeking your further support.

Each section is short so that children will be able to complete the activities you select in the time available. The homework book is available for those who finish early and wish to keep busy, as well as for work outside the classroom. Other activities which the children may do during this time are independent reading and preparing presentations for the class.

It is suggested that you aim to work with each guided reading and writing group for two sessions per week, organised so that you see each child in the class at least once.

Plenary

The final 10 minutes of the literacy hour is a plenary session for reviewing, reflecting upon, consolidating teaching points and presenting work covered in the lesson. This is an essential element of the hour. It is important to plan this activity so that every child has the opportunity to feed back once as part of their group during the course of a week. A different objective will be featured each day so that each objective is reinforced in turn. This will allow you to monitor each group's progress and highlight the teaching/learning points as necessary.

Using *Focus On Literacy*

The Big Book anthologies

There are three Big Book anthologies, each covering a term's work. These consist of carefully chosen texts for shared work on text, word and sentence levels. The extracts also provide the context for the independent activities. Each unit provides texts for a week's shared reading.

Each extract in the anthology begins with a short introduction, placing the text that follows in context. The extract is accompanied by a *To think and talk about* section to prompt and stimulate the children's responses.

Further teaching points and suggestions are given in the Teacher's Resource Book.

The Pupil's Book

The Pupil's Book is made up of thirty units. Each unit begins with the main text and is followed by the independent activities for the week.

To help you with differentiation, the independent activities are identified for level of difficulty, section A being the easiest and D the hardest. Each section is scaled to a workable size. By matching the level of difficulty to a group's ability level, you can help assure that children can complete the activities in the time available.

The five-day spread

The independent activity for **Day 1** is text-based. Section A has questions for literal recall, while those in section B are inferential. These independent questions are in addition to those in the *To think and talk about* section, which are intended as shared reading questions in order for you to help the children to explore the text at greater depth.

Day 2 independent activities focus on word, sentence or text work.

Day 3 begins with shared writing, followed by independent writing.

Day 4 is the same as Day 3.

Day 5 completes the word, sentence or text work.

'Stickers' provide the children with the facts they need to complete the work and make the most of the activities.

The Homework Book

The Homework Book contains activities which consolidate and extend the work in the pupil's book. This book is equally useful in the classroom outside the literacy hour and out of the classroom for work at home.

The Teacher's Resource Book

The Teacher's Resource Book comprises notes, copymasters, assessment masters, record-keeping sheets and NLS charts. It also outlines a basic approach to each unit in the Big Books and Pupil's Books and includes a reward certificate.

The teacher's notes and you

The teacher's notes help you use the ***Focus on Literacy*** material to the best advantage. The notes are arranged in five sections, each covering one literacy hour. These are further subdivided according to the literacy format: shared text/shared writing work, focused word/sentence work, independent work, and plenary.

A termly planning chart introduces each group of ten units. This chart lists the range of texts for that term, the text, sentence and word work which is explicitly covered, and the continuous work which will be part of your teaching throughout the term, such as practising reading and spelling strategies.

The teacher's notes for each text are organised to facilitate the literacy hour.

A *Key Learning Objectives* box lists the key literacy objectives covered in that week's work and a Resources box identifies the range of texts covered, details of the extracts and the page references of all the components used in the unit.

Details are given of any special preparation you need to do for the unit, for example, providing dictionaries.

The *Shared reading* section lists teaching points and suggestions on how to explore the meaning of the text, in line with the literacy framework objectives. In fiction and poetry this entails exploring genres, settings, characters, plots, themes, figurative language, authorship and the way different texts are organised. In non-fiction text this involves genres, structures and presentation, identifying main points, skimming and scanning, following an argument, exploring steps in a process, comparing different sources and differentiating fact, opinion and persuasion.

The texts often provide both structure and content for writing activities, and the context for many of the activities at sentence and word level on the copymasters.

The *Shared writing* section offers guidance on how texts are composed. The main text studied in earlier shared reading sessions will provide the ideas and structure for this writing. Each shared writing activity is the starting point for subsequent independent writing.

The *Focused sentence/word work* section offers appropriate teaching points and suggestions for investigating text in detail to explore how its message is influenced by style: language, grammar, choice of vocabulary and presentation. The Pupil's Book supports independent consolidation of the work.

The *Independent work* section introduces the independent reading, writing or word and sentence activities which may be found in the Pupil's Book, the Homework Book or on copymasters.

The *Plenary* section has suggestions for reviewing and reflecting upon the work covered, consolidating teaching points and presenting work, among others.

A *Consolidation and extension* section has ideas and suggestions for follow-up activities.

The *Homework* section describes the related activity in the Homework Book.

Copymasters

The copymasters offer a range of support material among which are book reviews, planning sheets, charts for collecting and classifying words, consolidation and extension work.

Assessment

To facilitate assessment there is an assessment master for each term, and a self-assessment master for the year's work.

Record keeping

Record-keeping sheets are provided at the back of the resource book. They feature a summary of the term's objectives, each with a space for your comments.

Award certificate

A photocopiable award certificate is provided to reward significant individual achievements in literacy.

NLS charts

A chart listing all literacy objectives for the year, and showing how these are covered by ***Focus on Literacy*** materials, is included in the back of the resource book.

Basic approach to each unit

The basic approach to each unit in ***Focus on Literacy*** is as follows:

Day 1

Shared **reading** of the week's main text in the anthology.

Focused word/sentence work based on the main text.

Independent text work on the main text, which is reproduced in the pupil's book.

Plenary session for which there are suggestions in the teacher's notes.

Day 2

Further shared **reading** of the main text.

Further focused word/sentence work based on the main text.

Independent word, sentence or text work in the pupil's book.

Plenary suggestions in the teacher's notes.

Day 3

Shared **writing**, using the main text as a model or stimulus.

Focused word/sentence work, appropriate to the shared writing task.

Independent writing, using guidance in the pupil's book.

Plenary suggestions in the teacher's notes.

Day 4

Shared **reading** of the second text in the anthology.

Focused word/sentence work based on the second text.

Continuation of the independent writing from Day 3.

Plenary suggestions in the teacher's notes.

Day 5

Further shared **reading** of the second text.

Focused word/sentence work based on the second text.

Independent word, sentence or text work in the pupil's book.

Plenary suggestions in the teacher's notes.

This approach is flexible, occasionally varied to make the most of the week's activities. For example, the shared reading for Day 4 might be replaced by shared writing when more extended written work is being developed; shared writing might begin on Day 2; or the second text might be shared on Day 2.

Work outside the literacy hour

The copymasters and homework book provide activities for outside the literacy hour and outside the classroom.

The extracts in ***Focus on Literacy*** are only part of the genre coverage. You will need time outside of the literacy hour to read aloud to your class, giving children the opportunity to hear complete stories, novels and poems. You will also need to show them complete non-fiction texts, so that features such as covers, blurbs, information about authors, contents, indices and chapter headings can be discussed and appreciated. Children will need further time for their own independent reading for interest and pleasure, and older pupils will need time for extended writing.

You can help to reinforce genre features when children choose books for independent reading, or during guided reading sessions when you are working with a group.

Big Book contents

BIG BOOK 4A TERM 1

BIG BOOK 4B TERM 2

BIG BOOK 4C TERM 3

Pupil's Book contents

TERM 1

TERM 2

TERM 3

Homework Book contents

TERM 1

TERM 2

TERM 3

Copymasters checklist

TERM 1

	Copymaster	
Unit 1	1	Fiction book review: introduction, build up, main event, ending
	2	Planning a story: introduction, build up, main event, ending
	3	A book thermometer: charting the interest level
Unit 2	4	Finding out about writers
Unit 4	5	How to . . . write, find information, learn to spell (reference sheet)
	6, 7	Glossary of language terms
Unit 7	8	Writing frame: a playscript
Unit 8	9	Message in a bottle: writing a message
Unit 10	10	Collecting rhymes
	11	Revision: assessment master for Term 1

TERM 2

Unit 11	12	Presentation master for description of cellar
Unit 13	13	Collecting adjectives
Unit 14	14	Presentation master for description
Unit 15	15	Words which are little used
Unit 16	16	Finding out: planning sheet
	17	Finding out: finding and recording information
Unit 19	18	Presentation master: sea shell poem
	19	Descriptive writing
Unit 20	20	Revision: assessment master for Term 2

TERM 3

Unit 21	21	Reading record
Unit 22	22	Comparing books by the same author
Unit 23	23	Book review: a story that raises an isssue
	24	Book review: plot – build-up, climax and ending
Unit 25	25	Words linked by spelling and meaning
Unit 26	26	Writing frame: expressing an opinion on keeping pets
Unit 29	27	Looking at adverts
	28	Writing an advert
Unit 30	29	Self-assessment master: How am I getting on?
	30	Revision: assessment master for Term 3

Focus on Literacy Achievement Award

Record sheets: Year 4, Term 1
Year 4, Term 2
Year 4, Term 3

Teacher's Notes

Year 4 • Terms 1–3

HALF-TERMLY PLANNER

Year 4 • Term 1 • Weeks 1–5

SCHOOL ________________ **CLASS** ________ **TEACHER** ____________

		Phonetics, spelling and vocabulary	Grammar and punctuation	Comprehension and composition	Texts
Continuous work **Weeks 1–5**		WL 1, 2, 3, 4, 10, 15, 17	SL 1	TL 23	**Range** **Fiction and poetry:** historical stories and short novels **Non-fiction:** instructions, information text
Blocked work					
Week	**Unit**				**Titles**
1	**1**	WL 6, 7	SL 2, 3	TL 1, 2, 3, 4, 9, 10, 15	extracts from *Blitz*, Robert Westall
2	**2**	—	SL 4, 5	TL 1, 2, 8, 11	extracts from *Street Child*, Berlie Doherty
3	**3**	WL 7, 8	SL 2	TL 1, 2, 3, 4, 9, 10, 12, 15	extracts from *Cue for Treason*, Geoffrey Trease
4	**4**	WL 5, 9, 11	—	TL 1, 10, 12, 15, 16, 17	information text: 'The Great Plague' and an extract from *A Parcel of Patterns*, Jill Paton Walsh
5	**5**	WL 12,14	SL 1	TL 18, 22, 25, 26	extracts from *Chocolate*, Jacqueline Dineen and *Usborne Complete Book of Home Magic*, Cheryl Evans and Ian Keable-Elliott

Focus on Literacy Teacher's Resource Book 4 © Barry and Anita Scholes, HarperCollins*Publishers* Ltd 1999

HALF-TERMLY PLANNER

Year 4 • Term 1 • Weeks 6–10

SCHOOL ______________ **CLASS** ________ **TEACHER** ______________

		Phonetics, spelling and vocabulary	Grammar and punctuation	Comprehension and composition	Texts
Continuous work Weeks 6–10		WL 1, 2, 3, 4, 10, 15, 16, 17	SL 1, 2		**Range** **Fiction and poetry:** poems based on common themes: animals, school **Non-fiction:** a range of text types from reports and articles in newspapers and magazines
Blocked work **Week**	**Unit**				**Titles**
6	**6**	WL 11, 13	SL 4	TL 7, 14	poems: 'Animals' Houses', James Reeves; 'The Guppy', Ogden Nash; 'Jump or Jiggle', Evelyn Beyer; 'Mice', Rose Fyleman; 'Cat', Mary Britton Miller; 'Cats', Eleanor Farjeon
7	**7**	—	SL 3, 4	TL 5, 6, 13	extracts from *All Aboard the Ark*, Sheila Lane and Marion Kemp
8	**8**	WL 6, 11, 12	SL 1, 4, 5	TL 18, 19, 20, 21, 23, 24	newspaper reports: 'The 10,000-mile message in a bottle', *Daily Mail*; 'An alien? Fat Chance', *Daily Mail*; 'Token that took 28 years to cash in', *Daily Mail*; 'What's up duck?', *Oldham Advertiser*
9	**9**	WL 8	SL 2, 4	TL 18, 19, 20, 21, 24, 27	newspaper reports: 'The postman's spat with a black and white cat', *The Express*; 'Houseplants'; 'Weather forecast'; 'Classified Ad'
10	**10**	WL 8, 13	SL 2	TL 7, 14	poems: 'I Went Back', Gwen Dunn; 'He who owns the whistle rules the world', Roger McGough; 'Out of School', Hal Summers; 'Mr Fitzsimmons', Stanley Cook

Unit 1 Air Raid

Key Learning Objectives

TL1	To investigate how settings and characters are built up from small details, and how the reader responds to them
TL2	To identify the main characteristics of the key characters, drawing on the text to justify views, and using the information to predict actions
TL3	To explore chronology in narrative, using written or other media texts
TL4	To explore narrative order
TL9	To use different ways of planning stories
TL10	To plan a story identifying the stages of its telling
TL15	To use paragraphs in story writing to organise and sequence narrative
SL2	To revise work on verbs from Year 1 Term 3 and to investigate verb tenses To understand the term 'tense' To understand that one test of whether a word is a verb is whether or not its tense can be changed
SL3	To identify the use of powerful verbs
WL6	To distinguish between the spelling and meanings of the homophones *of/off*
WL7	To spell regular verb endings, *s, ed, ing*

Range:	historical stories
Texts:	Extracts from *Blitz*, Robert Westall, Collins (also available as a Collins cassette tape)
Resources:	Big Book 4A pp.4-7 Pupil's Book 4 pp.2-4 Homework Book 4 p.2: Homophones: *there/their/they're; his/is* Copymaster 1: Fiction book review Copymaster 2: Planning a story Copymaster 3: A book thermometer: charting how a story is built up

DAY 1

Big Book 4A pp.4-5; Pupil's Book p.2-3

Shared reading

- Introduce the children to the historical context: World War 2 (1939-45),with particular reference to the German air raids of British ports, manufacturing centres, cities, etc. Then read the first extract in the anthology.
- Investigate how the setting of this extract is built up. Which words and phrases set the scene?
- What do the boys say which reveals that they are familiar with air raids? What is it that they have not experienced before?
- What does the class think of the behaviour of the boys? Should they have gone to find the crashed plane? What dangers might there be?
- Why are the boys reluctant to say what might have happened to the pilot? What are they 'expecting to find at every corner'? What would the class do next if they were the boys in the story?

Focused word/sentence work

- Revise verbs. Ask the children to pick out examples from the text. Ask which are strong verbs, e.g. streaking, howling, screaming, sparking.
- Revise the term 'tense'. In which tense is this narrative written? Look for examples of present verbs, e.g. 'there they go', 'where is it, then?' Why is the present tense used only in the dialogue?
- Explain that one test of whether a word is a verb or not is whether its tense can be changed. Explore this with words of different parts of speech, e.g. boy, big, tiptoe, farmer, look, pilot, long, dig, surprisingly, open, terrible, blue.

Independent work

- Children work on the comprehension questions on page 3 of the pupil's book. To help with differentiation the work is in two sections. Section A is literal (recognition or recall of detail), while section B is inferential (deducing answers where information is not given directly) or speculative.

Plenary

- Review the children's independent text work. Explain how to use the text to find literal answers, and how to use clues where information is not given directly.

DAY 2

Big Book 4A pp.4-5; Pupil's Book p.3

Shared reading

- Explore how the writer builds up the tension during the extract, by concentrating mainly on sound. At first the boys can see only the planes, but then they hear the machine-guns. How does the author describe the sound? How is the sound of the Heinkel described? What effect did it have on the boys? This is followed by the sound of the crash. How is that described? What is the effect of the line 'Then silence'? How do the previous descriptions of sound make this particularly effective?
- What smell is described?
- How do the boys feel as they realise the crashed plane is British? Which words describe this?
- What does the class think 'Kor' might be?

Focused word/sentence work

- Explain that tense may be past, present or future. Ask the children to look for examples of the future tense, e.g. 'if the guns don't get them the fighters will'.
- Experiment with changing one tense to another.
- Explore the use in the passage of the word *of*, e.g. 'the funnels of the ships', a row of iron railings'. How is *of* different from *off*? Ask the children to give examples of the use of both words. Encourage them to discover differences in meaning and use.

Independent work

- Children work on verb tense, and the homophones *of/off* on page 3 of the pupil's book.

Plenary

- Review the children's independent work. Consolidate teaching points, clarifying any misconceptions.

DAY 3

Big Book 4A pp.4-5; Pupil's Book p.4

Shared reading/writing including focused word/sentence work

- Discuss the chronology of the extract: the introduction describing the setting, the build-up as they watch the planes and hear the loud noise of the Heinkel, leading to the crash itself and the realisation that the plane is British.
- Identify the words and phrases which signal time, e.g. 'at that moment', 'then silence'. Notice that the long search for the plane is skimmed over in the words 'It took a long time to search ruined Kor.'
- Look at the planning notes on page 4 in the pupil's book. Discuss how the story of an accident can be planned in four paragraphs: introduction, build-up, main event (climax) and ending (resolution).
- Discuss how sound might play an important part in the story, as it does in the extract from *Blitz*.
- Show how stories can be planned in a number of ways. Brainstorm ideas. Make notes. Draw a diagram to show the accident: the road, the ditch, the hill, the trees, the fenced field. Discuss ways of marking the route of the car, where the children were when they heard it, where they were forced into the ditch and where the car crashed through the fence and came to a stop.
- Look at Copymaster 1, which is a book review, to explore the main stages of a story.
- Use Copymaster 2 as a planning sheet to help with the main stages of the children's own story writing.
- Look at Copymaster 3 which is a 'book thermometer'. This is a book mark which the children may use to record the 'excitement level' of each chapter of a story book. It will help them understand how stories build up to climaxes and resolutions (see Consolidation and extension).

Independent work

- Children begin independent writing.

Plenary

- Review the work in progress, offering help and encouragement.

DAY 4

Big Book 4A pp.6-7; Pupil's Book p.4

Shared reading

- Read the continuation of the tale in the second extract from *Blitz* in the anthology.
- Explore how the suspense is built up from small details: the new row of furrows in the farmer's field, the gap in the hedge, the lump of tail, and finally the Hurricane itself 'as big as a house'.
- What further detail are we given?

Focused word/sentence work

- Pick out the verbs in the text. Which are strong verbs?
- Experiment with changing verbs in the story. What effect does this have on meaning?

Independent work

- Children continue their writing.

Plenary

- Ask the children to read aloud their completed stories to the class. Draw the children's attention to good examples of introductions, build-ups, etc.

DAY 5

Big Book 4A pp.4-7; Pupil's Book p.4

Shared reading

- Why has the author chosen not to complete the second and last sentences in the extract? How might these be completed?
- Which sentence in the previous extract has not been completed? Why?
- Which character says, 'Hurricane, you idiot.'? Is it the narrator or Albert? How can the children tell? What else shows that this boy is the most knowledgeable?
- What would the children do next if they were the boys in the story? Why? What might the consequences be?

Focused word/sentence work

- Discuss how *-ing* can be added to a verb, e.g. searching, vanishing, flying, taking. Ask what spelling rules there are when adding *-ing*, e.g. dropping the final 'e' (exploring), doubling some final consonants (trapping).
- Explore the past, present and future tenses of verbs with *-ing*, e.g. is flying, was flying, will be flying.
- Experiment with changing tenses.

Independent work

- Children practise using the *-ing* form of verbs.

Plenary

- Review the week's work, consolidating teaching points.

Consolidation and extension

- Ask the children to read their stories aloud to the class.
- Look again at Copymaster 1 to explore the main stages of a story.
- Copymaster 2 will to help with planning the main stages of the children's own story writing.
- The children may use Copymaster 3, the 'book thermometer', to record the 'excitement level' of each chapter of a story book. It will help them understand how stories build up to climaxes and resolutions. When a number of books have been recorded in this way, it will be interesting to compare the 'thermometers', especially on books by the same author.

Homework

- Page 2 in the homework book focuses on the homonyms *there/their/they're* and *his/is*.

Unit 2 Street Child

Key Learning Objectives

TL1	To investigate how settings and characters are built up from small details, and how the reader responds to them
TL2	To identify the main characteristics of the key characters, drawing on the text to justify views, and using the information to predict actions
TL8	To find out more about popular authors, poets, etc.
TL11	To write character sketches
SL4	To identify adverbs and understand their functions in sentences
SL5	To practise using commas to mark grammatical boundaries within sentences

Range: Historical stories and short novels
Texts: Extracts from *Street Child*, Berlie Doherty
Resources: Big Book 4A pp.8-12
Pupil's Book 4 pp.5-7
Homework Book 4 p.3: Adverbs
Copymaster 4: Finding out about writers

DAY 1

Big Book 4A pp.8-10; Pupil's Book p.5-6

Shared reading

- Introduce the children to the historical context, explaining how James Jarvis (Jim in the book) inspired Dr Barnardo (Barnie) to set up his famous refuge. Discuss the plight of homeless children in Victorian times.
- Read the first extract in the anthology. Investigate the setting. Encourage the children to pick out words and phrases which describe it, e.g. 'the spitting of the logs' inside and 'the bleak voice of the wind' outside.
- Explore chronology in the text. How is the passage of time shown as Barnie ponders the plight of Jim and the other boys? How does the writer indicate the change of scene and time between the school and the market?

Focused word/sentence work

- Investigate the use of commas to mark grammatical boundaries in the text.
- Investigate verb tense. Ask the children to identify examples of past, present and future tense.
- Ask the children to look for strong verbs, e.g. stare, insisted, drumming. Experiment with substituting alternative verbs. How is the meaning changed?

Independent work

- Children answer the questions on page 3 of the pupil's book about the text.

Plenary

- Review the children's independent text work. Explain how to use the text to find literal answers, and how to use clues where information is not given directly.

DAY 2

Big Book 4A pp.8-10; Pupil's Book p.6

Shared reading

- Investigate how the characters of Jim and Barnie are revealed to the reader. Ask the children to pick out the details.
- What do the children think of the two characters? What makes them think this?
- Ask the children to retell the story from the different points of view of Jim and Barnie.

Focused word/sentence work

- Ask the children to identify the adverbs 'anxiously' and 'slowly' in the text. Which verbs do they tell us more about?
- Discuss the impact of the adverbs on the text, by experimenting with deletion and substitution.
- Ask the children to identify adjectives in the text. Make a list, e.g. impatient, angry, whiney, great, quiet, etc.
- Investigate how many of the adjectives can be made into adverbs by adding the suffix *-ly*, e.g. impatiently, angrily, greatly, etc. Point out that words ending in *y* change the *y* to *i* before adding *-ly*.
- Ask the children to put into sentences the adverbs they have made.

Independent work

- Children identify adverbs, on page 6 of the pupil's book, practise making them from adjectives by adding *-ly*, and use them in sentences.

Plenary

- Review the children's work on adverbs, re-emphasising teaching points and clarifying misconceptions.

DAY 3

Big Book 4A pp.8-10; Pupil's Book p.7

Shared reading/writing, including focused word/sentence work

- Ask the children to identify the main characteristics of the two characters.
- Discuss which words and phrases in the text build up the characters.
- Ask why Jim is uncertain what to do at the end of the extract. What do the children think he will decide? What might Barnie do then?
- Look at the section on sketching a character,'Jim and Barnie', on page 7 in the pupil's book. Discuss answers to the questions on Jim and Barnie. Encourage the children to express their personal response to each one. Use the children's responses to make notes on each character.
- The children plan a letter telling a friend about one of the characters, using the plan to structure ideas.
- Remind the children how to set out a letter.

Independent work

- Children write their letters about either Jim or Barnie. They will write their letters about the other character on day 4.

Plenary

- Ask some children to read out their letters. Provide feedback and encouragement.

DAY 4

Big Book 4A pp.11-12; Pupil's Book p.7

Shared reading

- Read the further extract from *Street Child* on pages 11-12 in the anthology. Is this how the children expected the story to continue?
- What was it Barnie seemed to understand about Jim?
- Why is Jim so upset that he has told Barnie his name? What does this tell us about Jim?

Focused word/sentence work

- Ask the children to identify a word with the suffix *-al* (special). Ask them to use the word in a sentence of their own. Ask how many other words they can think of which end with the same suffix, e.g. historical, signal, final, personal, festival.
- What parts of speech are the *-al* words they found? Test for nouns by whether they can be pluralised and for verbs by the tense change test. How many of the words can be made into adverbs by adding *-lie*? What part of speech are those words?

Independent work

- Children write a letter about the second character.

Plenary

- Review the children's letters, offering help and encouragement.

DAY 5

Big Book 4A pp.8-12; Pupil's Book p.7

Shared reading

- How can we tell that Jim is used to climbing, but Barnie isn't?
- Which details tell us that the wall had been climbed many times?
- What does 'sleeping like dogs' mean?
- Ask the children to retell this part of the story from the different points of view of Jim and Barnie.
- What does the class think will happen next? What makes them think this?

Focused word/sentence work

- Investigate the use of commas to mark grammatical boundaries within sentences in the text.
- Demonstrate by reading aloud that commas come where the reader ought to pause when reading.
- Revise the use of commas to separate words and phrases in a list. Play the 'I went to market and bought...' game in which children in turn add an item to a list of things bought at the market. Each child has to remember the complete list to date and then add another purchase, or drop out. Encourage the children to sound out the commas in the list, e.g. I went to the market and bought apples (comma) potatoes (comma), etc.

Independent work

- Children practise the use of commas on page 7 in the pupil's book.

Plenary

- Review the week's work, re-emphasising teaching points and clarifying misconceptions.

Consolidation and extension

- Display the children's letters about Jim and Barnie.
- Copymaster 4 helps the children to find out more about authors and poets. Discuss where they may find such information, e.g. book covers, TV and magazine features, by writing to them, etc. Encourage them to use this information to move onto more books by favourite writers.

Homework

- Page 3 in the homework book consolidates work on adverbs.

Unit 3 Besieged

Key Learning Objectives

TL1	To investigate how settings and characters are built up from small details, and how the reader responds to them
TL2	To identify the main characteristics of the key characters, drawing on the text to justify views, and using the information to predict actions
TL3	To explore chronology in narrative
TL4	To explore narrative order
TL9	To use different ways of planning stories
TL10	To plan a story identifying the stages of its telling
TL12	To write independently, linking own experience to situations in historical stories
TL15	To use paragraphs in story writing to organise and sequence narrative
SL2	To investigate verb tenses
WL7	To spell regular verb endings, *s, ed, ing*
WL8	To spell irregular tense changes

Range:	Historical novels and stories
Texts:	Extracts from *Cue for Treason*, Geoffrey Trease
Resources:	Big Book 4A pp.13-17 Pupil's Book 4 pp.8-10 Homework Book 4 p.4: The past tense

DAY 1

Big Book 4A pp.13-14; Pupil's Book pp.8-9

Shared reading

- Introduce the children to the historical context: the time of Elizabeth 1. What details show that the story is not set in modern times?
- What details set the scene?
- Ask the children to explain what is happening in the story.
- What do we learn about the main characters in this extract: the narrator (Peter), his father and Sir Philip?
- What do the children think will happen next? How might the characters react?

Focused word/sentence work

- Encourage the children to use context clues to infer the meaning of new words, e.g. adversary, foppishly, sublimely, rapiers, breach.
- Identify the use of powerful verbs, e.g. growled, tramping, skirmished, danced, clutching. Experiment with alternatives, and discuss how this changes the meaning.
- Identify the *-ly* adverbs in the text, e.g. foppishly, slowly, tensely, hurriedly.

Independent work

- Children answer the comprehension questions on page 9 in the pupil's book.

Plenary

- Review the children's independent text work. Explain how to use the text to find literal answers, and how to use clues where information is not given directly.

DAY 2

Big Book 4A pp.13-14; Pupil's Book p.9

Shared reading

- Ask the children to retell the story in their own words.
- Explore the narrative order. Notice how, even within this short extract, we have a build-up and a conflict. Explore the build-up: Peter's going upstairs, the description of what he sees, the realisation of what they intend to do, his father's determination, followed by a period of waiting.
- Notice how the writer describes rather than skims over this period. What details does he give?
- The conflict in this part of the story is the attempt to use the battering ram. How is this particular incident resolved?

Focused word/sentence work

- Ask the children to identify examples of the past, present and future tenses.
- Investigate regular verb endings, e.g. go<u>ing</u>, graz<u>ing</u>, dismount<u>ed</u>, group<u>ed</u>.
- Discuss the spelling rules for adding these endings: verbs ending in *e* drop it before adding *-ing* or *ed*, e.g. grazing, grazed; some verbs double the last letter, e.g. strutted; verbs ending in *-y* change it to *i*, e.g. hurried.
- Explore *-ing* verb endings in present and past tenses, and the need for grammatical agreement, e.g. I am going, you are going, he is going.

Independent work

- Children explore verbs: *-ing* endings in present and past tenses, on page 9 of the pupil's book.

Plenary

- Review the children's independent work on verb tense. Re-emphasise teaching points and clarify any misconceptions.

DAY 3

Big Book 4A pp.13-17; Pupil's Book p.10

Shared writing

- Ask the children to retell the story from Peter's point of view.
- Ask what the extract tell us of how he feels, e.g. 'We waited tensely.' Ask them to imagine how he would feel at other points in the story.
- Read the continuation of the story on page 16 in the anthology.
- Ask the children to explain what Peter thinks will happen next. What do they think he will do then?

- Read and discuss the ideas and suggestions in the section on writing a story, 'Under siege' on page 10 of the pupil's book.
- Use details from both extracts to draw a sketch of the setting, showing how Sir Philip's men might be able to reach the door without being fired on.
- Develop these ideas into a story told from Peter's point of view. Plan the story in four paragraphs: introduction, build-up, conflict and resolution.

Focused word/sentence work

- In which person is the story told? Remind the children that their story from Peter's point of view will be written in the first person.
- Identify the strong verbs in the second extract, e.g. gesticulating, dashed, sneak, stooped.

Independent work

- Children begin their independent writing.

Plenary

- Review the children's writing in progress, offering help and encouragement.

DAY 4

Big Book 4A p.16; Pupil's Book p.10

Shared reading

- Read the second extract again.
- Explore the narrative order. Is this extract a build-up, a main event (climax or conflict) or a resolution? How can the children tell?

Focused word/sentence work

- Ask the children to check their own writing for grammatical errors, verb agreement, punctuation and spelling mistakes.
- Investigate the use of commas to mark grammatical boundaries within sentences.

Independent work

- Children continue their writing.

Plenary

- Ask the children to read aloud their stories. Draw attention to good story construction, use of words, etc.

DAY 5

Big Book 4A pp.13-17; Pupil's Book p.10

Shared reading

- Ask the children to retell the story, combining both extracts, from the different points of view of Peter's father and Sir Philip.
- Continue this by predicting, in character, what they will do next.

Focused word/sentence work

- Identify verbs in the passage with regular endings, e.g. announced, dashed, grabbed, hauled. Notice the double letters in 'grabbed'.
- Investigate irregular tense changes, e.g. caught. Look back at the earlier extract for other examples, e.g. ran, gave, saw, sang, drew.
- Ask the children to think of other irregular verbs. Make a list.

Independent work

- Children explore regular and irregular tense changes.

Plenary

- Review the children's independent work.
- Re-emphasise the week's main teaching points.

Consolidation and extension

- Encourage the children to use a word processor for the final drafts of their stories.
- Record the best of these on tape.
- Design a cover for the cassette.
- Design a poster to advertise the cassette.

Homework

- Page 4 in the homework book consolidates understanding of regular and irregular tense changes.

Unit 4 The Great Plague

Key Learning Objectives

TL1	To investigate how settings and characters are built up from small details, and how the reader responds to them
TL10	To plan a story identifying the stages of its telling
TL12	To write independently, linking own experience to situations in historical stories
TL15	To use paragraphs in story writing to organise and sequence narrative
TL16	To identify different types of non-fiction text
TL17	To identify features of non-fiction texts
WL5	To spell two-syllable words containing double consonants
WL9	To recognise and spell the suffixes: *-al, -ary, -ic, -ship, -hood, -ness, -ment*
WL11	To define familiar vocabulary in their own words

Range:	Information text; historical story
Texts:	'The Great Plague' (information text) Extract from *A Parcel of Patterns*, Jill Paton Walsh
Resources:	Big Book 4A pp.18-23 Pupil's Book 4 pp.11-13 Homework Book 4 p.5: Double consonants Copymaster 5: How to... write, find information, learn to spell Copymasters 6 and 7: Glossary of language terms for children

Preparation

- Make available background material about the Great Plague of 1665.
- A dictionary will be required on day 5, preferably *Collins Junior Dictionary*.

DAY 1

Big Book 4A pp.18-21; Pupil's Book pp.11-12

Shared reading

- Introduce the children to the Tudor world of 1665 and the Great Plague.
- Read and discuss the text. Emphasise that no one at the time knew what caused the plague, and no effective medicine existed.
- Examine what the people of the time did to avoid the disease. How effective would these precautions have been?
- If people had understood how the disease was spread, what different precautions might they have taken?
- Discuss how the list of symptoms shows the progress of the disease.
- How does the text give us information about doctors? What do the children think about the doctors' special outfits? Might this have kept them safe from the plague? What effect might it have had on the patients?
- When they are answering the questions in the 'To Think and Talk About' section, ask the children to use the underlined key words.

Focused word/sentence work

- Investigate the verbs in the passage. What tense are they? What tense are the verbs in the separate 'Symptoms' box? Why is this different?
- Experiment with substituting different verbs which preserve the meaning, e.g. 'came' for 'arrived', 'passed on' or 'transmitted' for 'spread', etc.
- Ask which adverbs the children can find, e.g. quickly, completely. Can the children think of alternative adverbs with the same meaning?

Independent work

- Children answer the questions in the pupil's book on page 12 about the Great Plague passage.

Plenary

- Review the children's independent text work.

DAY 2

Big Book 4A pp.18-21; Pupil's Book p.12

Shared reading

- What is the purpose of the text?
- Investigate its layout: headings, paragraphs, separate list of symptoms with bulleted points, illustration and caption. How do these help the reader?
- What person is the text written in?
- What special vocabulary does it use? What are the following: muscular pain, buboes, bacteria?

Focused word/sentence work

- Investigate how words can be built from other words with similar patterns, e.g. 'infection' from 'infect', 'development' from 'develop', 'medical' from 'medicine'.
- Explore the suffixes *-al* and *-ness* in words in the text: e.g. 'special', 'sickness'. Can the children think of other words with the same suffixes, e.g. animal, original, final, natural, goodness, badness, darkness, stillness, softness etc.
- Explore the suffixes *ment, -hood, -ary, -ic, -ship* in preparation for the children's independent work.

Independent work

- Children explore suffixes: *-ness, -ment, -hood, -al, -ary, -ic, -ship.*

Plenary

- Review the children's independent work. Make a classified list, according to suffix, of the words in section E on page 12 of the pupil's book.

DAY 3

Big Book 4A pp.18-21; Pupil's Book p.13

Shared reading/writing, including focused word/sentence work

- As you read the text again, ask the children to imagine what it must have been like to be living in London at the time of the Great Plague. Discuss how they would have responded to the situation.
- Use the suggestions on page 13 in the pupil's book to plan a story about being there. As you plan each paragraph encourage the children to refer to the text for detail which will set the story firmly in its historical context and bring it to life.
- Make a list of the sights, sounds and smells of the time.
- Discuss how the children would feel at different points in the story and what they might be thinking.
- What tense and person will be appropriate for this story? Why?
- Experiment with opening sentences which set the scene and capture interest.

Independent work

- Children begin writing their story.

Plenary

- Review the work in progress. Make sure the children are using information from *The Great Plague* text to add realism to their stories.

DAY 4

Big Book 4A p.22; Pupil's Book p.13

Shared reading

- Read the extract from *A Parcel of Patterns.* Explain that the plague did actually travel from London to the remote Derbyshire village of Eyam, probably in the parcel of dress patterns of the book's title.
- Ask which words tell us that this is a historical story, e.g. apothecary, stocks and farrier. What do these words mean?
- Which details build up the picture of the village. How does this explain the spread of the plague?
- How does the text make the children feel? Why?

Focused word/sentence work

- Ask the children to find examples of words with double consonants, e.g. middle, dwelling.
- Investigate the use of commas in the text.
- Children continue their stories.

Plenary

- Read aloud examples of the children's stories. Discuss features such as story structure, and factual detail. Choose children to prepare for reading their stories to the class on day 5.

DAY 5

Big Book 4A p.22; Pupil's Book p.13

Shared reading

- What is the main idea of each paragraph in the extract?
- How would Goody Trickett's garden of herbs normally have been useful in the absence of an apothecary and surgeon?
- Would the herbs, apothecary or surgeon have been effective in preventing or curing the plague? What makes you think so?
- Can you think how the villagers prevented the disease spreading to other villages?

Focused word/sentence work

- Ask the children to give definitions for selected words in the text, e.g. sickness, street, cottage, middle. Encourage them to check and refine their definitions. Compare them with dictionary definitions.

Independent work

- Children write their own definitions for familiar words on page 13 of the pupil's book.

Plenary

- Ask those children chosen on day 4 to read aloud their stories.

Consolidation and extension

- Encourage the children to illustrate their stories.
- Copymaster 5 is a reference sheet to help the children with the writing process, to learn spellings and to find information.
- Copymasters 6 and 7, when copied back to back and folded, will make a useful four-page glossary of language terms.

Homework

- Page 5 in the homework book explores two-syllable words with double consonants.

Unit 5

Instructions

Key Learning Objectives

TL18 To select and examine opening sentences that capture interest

TL22 To identify features of instructional texts

TL25 To write clear instructions

TL26 To improve the cohesion of written instructions and directions through the use of link phrases and organisational devices

SL1 To re-read own writing to check for grammatical sense and accuracy

WL12 To use 3rd and 4th place letters to locate and sequence words in alphabetical order

WL14 To explore the ways in which nouns and adjectives can be made into verbs by use of the suffixes: *-ate, -ify, -en -ise.*

Range:	Instructions
Texts:	Recipe for a chocolate cake from *Chocolate*, Jacqueline Dineen and 'Book Test' from *Usborne Complete Book of Home Magic*, Cheryl Evans and Ian Keable-Elliott
Resources:	Big Book 4A pp.24-27 Pupil's Book 4 pp.14-16 Homework Book 4 p.6: More confusing words: *here/hear, new/knew*, etc.

Preparation

- Although it is not essential to follow the recipe for chocolate cake, it will greatly help the children to appreciate instructions if you do so. Please check with the recipe in the anthology and pupil's book for the ingredients. Making the cake may be done outside the literacy hour.

DAY 1

Big Book 4A pp.24-25; Pupil's Book p.14-15

Shared reading

- Read the recipe. Discuss its structure: headings, list of materials/ingredients, numbered points in sequence, illustrations, etc.
- How do these features make it easy to follow the recipe?
- How does the opening sentence capture interest?
- Ask how the recipe might be improved, e.g. a list of equipment: 17.5cm round tin, greaseproof paper, sieve, etc.

Focused word/sentence work

- Investigate homophones in the text: e.g. flour, two, pour, hour, plain, break, piece, some, need. Ask the children to identify the other halves of the homophone pairs, e.g. flower, plane, our, brake, etc.
- Encourage the children to use the homophones in sentences to show their meaning.
- Give the children sentences containing homophones and challenge them to give the correct spellings.

Independent work

- Children answer questions about the recipe on page 15 in the pupil's book.

Plenary

- Review the children's independent text work. Revise how to find answers from the text.

DAY 2

Big Book 4A pp.24-25; Pupil's Book p.15

Shared reading

- Investigate how the numbered steps take the place of paragraphs in other texts.
- Ask the children to suggest the main idea of each step, e.g. 1. preparation of the baking tin, 2. preparing the mixture, etc.
- What is the main idea of the first part of the recipe (steps 1-3), and of the second part (steps 4-6)?

Focused word/sentence work

- Sort the list of ingredients for the chocolate cake into alphabetical order. Remind the children how to do this by using the second letter when two words begin with the same letter, e.g. cream of tartar and caster sugar.
- Ask the children to suggest how to alphabetise words which have the same first two or three letters. Practise this.
- Revise homophones in preparation for the independent work.

Independent work

- Children explore alphabetical order to the 3rd and 4th letter on page 15 of the pupil's book.
- Children also investigate homophones.

Plenary

- Review the children's work on homophones, re-emphasising teaching points and clarifying misconceptions.

DAY 3

Big Book 4A pp.24-25; Pupil's Book p.16

Shared reading/writing, including focused word/sentence work

- Read the recipe again, re-emphasising its structural features: headings, list of materials/ingredients, numbered points in sequence, illustrations, etc.
- Pick out the verbs in the recipe. Which tense are they? Which person?
- These verbs are common in recipes: beat, mix, pour, bake, stir, spread, etc. Ask the children if they can think of any other common recipe verbs, e.g. fold, blend, slice, chop, etc.
- Compare this instructional text with a fiction or information text. How is it different? Develop awareness of how verb tense and person relate to the purpose and audience of the text.

- Choose one of the suggestions on page 16 in the pupil's book, e.g. how to mend a bicycle puncture. This will give practice in writing instructions for a different kind of activity from food preparation.
- Discuss aspects such as purpose, audience, and structure. Plan and write the instructions together. Emphasise the need for correct sequence and clarity.
- Read through what you have written to check that everything is clear and that you have left nothing out.

Independent work

- Children choose one of the suggestions on page 16 in the pupil's book, and write their own instructions.

Plenary

- Review the work in progress, with particular emphasis on clarity and structural features: headings, statement of the intended outcome, list of materials/ingredients, numbered points in sequence, and use of imperative verbs (2nd person). Might the addition of illustrations improve the clarity?

DAY 4

Big Book 4A pp.26-27; Pupil's Book p.16

Shared reading

- Read the instructions for the mind-reading trick on page 26 in the anthology.
- How does the opening sentence capture interest?
- Discuss the structure of the text.
- Ask one of the children to try out the trick on the rest of the class, carefully following the instructions step by step.
- Does the trick work properly? If not, why not? Are the instructions clear? Were they understood properly? Were they followed correctly?
- The trick will work well with practice and as the children gain confidence.
- Ask other children to try the trick out on a partner.

Focused word/sentence work

- Ask the children to identify the verbs in the instructions. How many are powerful verbs, e.g. memorize, concentrate.
- Explore using alternative verbs.
- Ask the children to identify the adverbs in the text, e.g. casually. Delete them and discuss the change in effect. Why is the word 'casually' so important?

Independent work

- Children choose another of the suggestions on page 16 in the pupil's book, and write their instructions.

Plenary

- Review the work in progress, with particular emphasis on structural features and clarity.

DAY 5

Big Book 4A pp.24-27; Pupil's Book p.16

Shared reading

- Why is it necessary to have a selection of books for the mind-reading trick rather than just two?
- Why must the spectator stop you near the middle of the book? What might you do to ensure he does? Suppose he still does not stop you near the middle? Is the trick ruined, or can you think of a convincing way to make him start the selection again?
- Once the trick has been tried the children should be able to say which part is the most difficult to perform. Can they suggest ways of changing the instructions to help the magician at these points?
- Why might getting the word slightly wrong be more effective than getting it right?

Focused word/sentence work

- Ask the children to find a verb in the text which comes from the noun *memory*.
- How is it made? Explain that *-ise* is an acceptable alternative to *-ize* (e.g. memor<u>ise</u> or memor<u>ize</u> are equally correct).
- Discuss verbs connected with cooking which have been formed by adding a suffix to a noun or adjective, e.g. liquid<u>ise</u>, sweet<u>en</u>, solid<u>ify</u>.
- Experiment with making verbs by adding these suffixes: *-ise, -ify, -en, -ate.*
- Discuss the spelling rules which govern these changes, e.g. dropping *y* and *e* , e.g. memorise, simplify.

Independent work

- Children explore ways in which nouns and adjectives can be made into verbs by the suffixes *-ate, -en, -ify* and *-ise.*

Plenary

- Review the children's work on suffixes. Discuss the spelling rules which cover the patterns.

Consolidation and extension

- Arrange with another class, or classes, for one or more of the children to perform the mind-reading trick to an audience who has not read the instructions.

Homework

- Page 6 in the homework book explains the homophones *here/hear* and *new/ knew.*

Unit 6 Animal Poems

Key Learning Objectives

TL7 To compare and contrast poems on similar themes

TL14 To write poems based on personal or imagined experience linked to poems read

SL3 To identify the use of powerful verbs

WL11 To define familiar vocabulary in their own words, using alternative phrases or expressions

WL13 To use a rhyming dictionary

Range:	Poems based on a theme – animals
Texts:	'Animals' Houses', James Reeves; 'The Guppy', Ogden Nash; 'Jump or Jiggle', Evelyn Beyer; 'Mice', Rose Fyleman 'Cat', Mary Britton Miller; 'Cats', Eleanor Farjeon
Resources:	Big Book 4A pp.28-31 Pupil's Book 4 pp.17-19 Homework Book 4 p.7: Animal homes and families

Preparation

- A rhyming dictionary is useful for days 3 and 4.

DAY 1

Big Book 4A pp.28-29; Pupil's Book pp.17-18

Shared reading

Read and enjoy the poems on pages 28-29 in the anthology. Ask the children to answer the questions in the 'To Think and Talk About' section.

- Compare the rhyming patterns of poems. How are they similar and different?
- Compare the patterns of the poems. How are they set out? How many verses? How long are the lines? How are they punctuated?
- Compare their rhythms.

Focused word/sentence work

- What tense are the verbs in each poem?
- What person are the verbs?
- What is the home of a cow? What animals live in kennels and sties?
- Do bats really have bittens? Why does Ogden Nash say they do?
- Ask the children to find the names of the young of other creatures, e.g. goats, cows, eagles, tigers, geese.

Independent work

- Children answer questions on the poems.

Plenary

- Review the children's independent text work.

DAY 2

Big Book 4A pp.28-29; Pupil's Book p.18

Shared reading

- How do the different poems make the children feel?
- What different pictures do the poems make in the children's mind? Which do they find the most/least pleasant? Why?
- Which poem do the children like best/least? Why?
- Ask the children to choose a poem to prepare for reading aloud on day 3.

Focused word/sentence work

- Identify the powerful and expressive verbs in 'Jump or Jiggle'. Ask the children if they can think of alternatives, e.g. frogs leap.
- Challenge the children to find expressive verbs for different animals, e.g. apes swing, cats steal, lambs frisk, wolves lope.

Independent work

- Children match 'powerful' verbs of movement to the creatures which make them, and use them in sentences.
- Children find, classify and use verbs for moving quickly and slowly. A thesaurus may be used for this activity. Suggest to the children that they look up synonyms for walk, run and move.

Plenary

- Review the children's independent work. Ask the children to put the verbs for walking slowly and quickly into order, slowest first.

DAY 3

Big Book 4A pp.28-29; Pupil's Book p.19

Shared reading/writing, including focused word/sentence work

- Ask the children to read aloud the poems they chose on day 2.
- Focus on the poems 'Jump or Jiggle' and 'Mice' as models for the children's own poems. Discuss the structure of each poem, and how it may be used or adapted.
- The children's poems do not need to rhyme, but you may wish to make the shared poem do so. Introduce the children to a rhyming dictionary and use it to find suitable rhymes. Emphasise that sense should always come before rhyme, except for special effect, e.g. in the Ogden Nash poem where the invented rhyme is funny precisely because it is puts rhyme before sense.
- Make a list of suitable words and phrases for the shared poem, including rhymes.
- Encourage the children to select ideas from the list for your shared poem.

Independent work

- Children choose one of the poems to use as a model for their own poem.

Plenary

- Review the work in progress, offering help and encouragement. Enjoy the children's completed poems in an atmosphere of constructive criticism.

DAY 4

Big Book 4A pp.30-31; Pupil's Book p.19

Shared reading

- Read the two poems on cats to the children once through, and then concentrate on each poem in turn.
- As you read the poem by Mary Britton Miller, ask the children to close their eyes and imagine the action described.
- The poem is like a film or a number of snapshots. The action it describes lasts only half a minute or so, but in that time every action of the cat is described in detail. Have the children seen cats behaving in this way? How accurate do they think the description is?
- Ask the children to pick out words and phrases which best describe the cat, and which made the clearest pictures in their minds. Which of these words are powerful verbs? Which are adjectives?
- How is the Eleanor Farjeon poem different? What pictures does it paint? How are the pictures different from those of the first poem? Are they as clear? Ask the children to justify their answers.
- Which poem did they like best? Why?

Focused word/sentence work

- Make a list of powerful and expressive verbs for the actions of cats, beginning with those from the poems. Keep a copy of the list for reference on day 5.

Independent work

- Children write a second poem.

Plenary

- Read aloud the children's poems, praising good use of powerful and expressive verbs.

DAY 5

Big Book 4A pp.28-31; Pupil's Book p.19

Shared reading

- Read again the two poems on cats on pages 30-31 in the anthology.
- Look at their forms. How are they similar? How are they different? Which is the list poem? How many verses do they have? Do they rhyme? What is the rhyming scheme? Encourage the children to tap out and compare their rhythms.
- How do the poems make the children feel?
- Ask the children to read the poems aloud.

Focused word/sentence work

- Return to your list of verbs for the actions of cats. Ask the children to suggest adverbs to describe each verb in your list, e.g. stand stiffly, pad softly. Discuss how these qualify the meaning of the verbs.
- Experiment with substitutions. How is the meaning affected? Which are the best adverbs? Why?

Independent work

- Children write their own definitions for common words. All the words can be found in the poems in this unit.

Plenary

- Review the week's work on powerful verbs and definitions, re-emphasising teaching points.

Consolidation and extension

- Compile the children's poems into an anthology. Add illustrations by the children.
- Encourage the children to record their poems on tape.
- Perform selected poems from this unit as choral speech.
- Encourage the children to find out more about popular children's poets such as James Reeves and Eleanor Farjeon.

Homework

- Page 7 in the homework book widens the children's vocabulary by exploring animals' homes and families.

Unit 7 Homeless!

Key Learning Objectives

TL5	To prepare, read and perform playscripts; compare organisation of scripts with stories
TL6	To chart the build-up of a play scene
TL13	To write playscripts
SL3	To identify the use of powerful verbs through cloze procedure
SL4	To identify adverbs and understand their functions in sentences

Range:	Playscripts
Texts:	Extracts from *All Aboard the Ark*, Sheila Lane and Marion Kemp
Resources:	Big Book 4A pp.32-35 Pupil's Book 4 pp.20-22 Homework Book 4 p.8: Correcting mistakes Copymaster 8: Writing frame: playscript

DAY 1

Big Book 4A pp.32-33; Pupil's Book pp.20-21

Shared reading

- Discuss the organisation of the playscript. Can the children think of reasons why the setting is not indicated? (This is an extract from a longer play, each scene taking place in the same setting.) How would the setting be indicated if this were the first scene?
- Examine how the dialogue is presented.
- How are the stage directions set out. How is the story line made clear?
- Ask the children to read the playscript aloud. Experiment with different ways of saying the lines.

Focused word/sentence work

- Discuss homophones in the text, e.g. 'hare' and 'hair', 'great' and 'grate', 'poor' and 'pour', 'tail' and 'tale', 'there' and 'their'. Encourage the children to distinguish between them by using them in sentences of their own.

Independent work

- Children answer the questions on the playscript.

Plenary

- Review the children's independent text work.

DAY 2

Big Book 4A pp.32-33; Pupil's Book p.21

Shared reading

- Ask children to read the playscript aloud.
- How is a playscript similar to, and different from, a story? Compare setting, story line, dialogue and the way action is described. How are we told the thoughts and feelings of characters in playscripts?
- Investigate the build up of the scene: beginning with action at a significant point in the story, using dialogue to describe action which is difficult to act out on stage, preparing for the entrance of the dormice (All listen . . . Sounds of screeching and squeaking), and building to a climax with all the dormice chorusing 'HOMELESS!'
- How are scenes usually concluded?
- How important are sounds in plays, especially off-stage ones?

Focused word/sentence work

- Ask the children to identify the adverbs in the text, e.g. properly, gently, wildly.
- Encourage them to suggest alternative adverbs.
- Ask them to suggest suitable adverbs to add to the stage directions, e.g. brushing fur vigorously, turning round quickly, springing into the air suddenly. What effect do the additional adverbs have?

Independent work

- Children work on adverbs, on page 21 in the pupil's book.

Plenary

- Review the children's independent work on adverbs. Consolidate teaching points, clarifying any misconceptions.

DAY 3

Big Book 4A pp.32-33; Pupil's Book p.22

Shared reading/writing, including focused word/sentence work

- Encourage the children to act out the playscript, following the stage directions.
- Explore the use of commas to mark grammatical boundaries in sentences, e.g. 'He comes barging along every morning, knocking everyone over'. Why is a comma used?
- Choose a story the children all know well for writing as a playscript. Select an exciting part of the story which is easily acted out.
- Use the suggestions and sample script in the pupil's book on page 22 to structure your ideas, and those of the class.

Independent work

- Children begin writing their own playscripts.
- Copymaster 8 is a writing frame to help the children set out the script.

Plenary

- Review the work in progress, offering help and encouragement.

DAY 4

Big Book 4A pp.34-35; Pupil's Book p.22

Shared reading

- Read the second extract from the playscript to the children.
- Which stage direction indicates the entrance of Bombo?
- Why is this an important entrance?
- What do the children think of Bombo?
- What does Hare mean when he says Bombo will have to be stopped? What does Bombo mean when he says, 'I have!'
- Ask the children to read the playscript aloud.

Focused word/sentence work

- Explore the use of adverbs in the text, e.g. wildly, kindly, firmly. Ask the children to read the appropriate lines in the manner of the adverbs.
- Explore alternatives for the adverbs, e.g. softly, angrily, despairingly. Ask the children to read in the manner of their suggestions.
- How important are adverbs in stage directions?

Independent work

- Children complete their own playscripts.

Plenary

- Review the children's playscripts.

DAY 5

Big Book 4A pp.32-35; Pupil's Book p.22

Shared reading

- Why are dots used in the script? Read the appropriate parts aloud to demonstrate their function. Ask the children to read aloud the same parts.
- Ask the children to act out the second extract from the script, or combine the two for a longer performance.
- How might the performance be improved?

Focused word/sentence work

- Investigate the use of powerful and expressive verbs in the text, e.g. sob, barging, flattened, trampled, lumbers. Ask the children to suggest alternatives.
- Look at the cloze passage on page 22 in the pupil's book. Encourage the children to think of suitable expressive verbs.

Independent work

- Children copy and complete the cloze passage.

Plenary

- Review the cloze passage. Discuss the effect of different verbs.

Consolidation and extension

- Ask the children to read aloud their own playscripts.
- Prepare a script for full performance.
- Copymaster 8 is a writing frame to help the children set out a playscript.

Homework

- Page 8 in the homework book gives practice in correcting errors in sentences: grammatical sense, agreement and spelling.

Unit 8

Read All About It!

Key Learning Objectives

TL18 To select and examine opening sentences that set scenes, capture interest, etc.; pick out key sentences/phrases that convey information

TL19 To understand and use the terms 'fact' and 'opinion', and distinguish the two

TL20 To identify main features of newspapers

TL21 To predict newspaper stories from the evidence of headlines, making notes, checking against original

TL23 To investigate how reading strategies are adapted to different properties of IT texts

TL24 To write newspaper style reports

SL1 To re-read own writing to check for grammatical sense and accuracy

SL4 To identify adverbs and understand their functions in sentences

SL5 To practise using commas to mark grammatical boundaries within sentences; link to work on editing and revising own writing

WL6 To distinguish between the spelling and meanings of common homophones

WL11 To define familiar vocabulary in their own words, using alternative phrases or expressions

WL12 To use 3rd and 4th place letters to locate and sequence words in alphabetical order

Range:	Newspaper reports
Texts:	'The 10,000-mile message in a bottle'; 'An alien? Fat Chance'; 'Token that took 28 years to cash in', *Daily Mail*; 'What's up duck?', *Oldham Advertiser*
Resources:	Big Book 4 pp.36-39 Pupil's Book 4A pp.23-25 Homework Book 4 p.9: Daily News – writing reports from headlines Copymaster 9: Message in a bottle – writing a message

Preparation

- Make available a number of newspapers for study throughout the week, especially on day 1.
- Collect suitable newspaper reports with headlines the children will find interesting. These will be useful on day 5.

DAY 1

Big Book 4A pp.36-37; Pupil's Book pp.23-24

Shared reading

- Look at a selection of newspapers (see 'Preparation' above). Identify the main features. Explore the layout: headings, columns, photographs and artwork. Consider the range of information: news reports, advertisements, weather forecasts, articles, etc.
- Read out the headlines from the reports on pages 36-37 in the anthology, but do not let the children refer to the reports. Ask them to predict what the stories might be about.
- Read the two news stories. How close are they to the children's predictions?
- Look at how the stories are organised: headlines, photograph, caption, columns and short paragraphs.

Focused word/sentence work

- Ask the children to identify the two-syllable words with double letters in the news reports, e.g. tossed, message, bottle. Encourage the children to use these words in sentences of their own.
- Investigate compound words, e.g. inside, someone, postman, football. Ask which words in the texts can be combined with other words to make compound words, e.g. over (overlook, takeover, overtake), up (upend, upside), moon (moonlight).

Independent work

- Children answer questions on the newspaper reports.

Plenary

- Review the children's independent text work, with particular emphasis on answers to questions in section B.

DAY 2

Big Book 4A pp.36-37; Pupil's Book p.24

Shared reading

- What is the main idea of each report?
- Encourage the children to suggest how the stories capture interest, e.g. headlines, pictures, opening sentence.
- Note that the short report on the whale blubber is a single sentence report. Challenge the children to give the main points of the bottle story in as few sentences as they can.
- Which sentences in the bottle story are the key ones which convey the bare bones of the story?
- Discuss the difference between fact and opinion. Ask the children to pick out one fact and one opinion from the whale blubber story. What is the pun in that story's headline?

Focused word/sentence work

- Ask the children to identify adverbs in the newspaper reports, e.g. neatly, promptly, incredibly, probably. Encourage them to use the words in sentences of their own.
- Identify words which are homophones, e.g. threw (through), not (knot), beach (beech), piece (peace), four (for), know (no). Encourage the children to use them in sentences which distinguish between them.

Independent work

- The independent work for day 2 is not differentiated in the usual way. Instead, there are six activities which cover a range of word, sentence and text level work. Sections 1 to 4 consolidate objectives covered in earlier units. Sections 5 and 6 are new work. Work may be assigned according to the needs of the children, perhaps with some activities reserved for outside the literacy hour, or as homework.

Plenary

- Review the children's independent work, re-emphasising teaching points and clarifying misconceptions.

DAY 3

Big Book 4A pp.36-37; Pupil's Book p.25

Shared writing, including focused word/sentence work

- Tell the children that you are going to produce together the front page of a newspaper, with two or three news stories. Discuss suitable subjects for a newspaper report: a school or local event, or an incident from a story.
- Select one of these ideas for your shared writing activity. Look at the list of reporter's question on page 25 in the pupil's book. These are questions to which your newspaper report should provide the answers. Make notes in true reporter fashion, listing the bare bones of the story.
- Discuss how to use these notes to construct a report. Refer to the suggestions in the pupil's book.
- Discuss suitable headlines. Write an opening sentence which sets the scene and captures interest, without giving too much of the story away at the outset.
- Write the news story together, using the anthology as a reference for style and organisation.
- Give the children practice in using commas to mark the grammatical boundaries within sentences.

Independent work

- Children write their own newspaper style report. This may be done on paper or using IT.

Plenary

- Review the work in progress. Do the reports provide answers to the reporter's questions listed in the pupil's book?

DAY 4

Big Book 4A pp.38-39; Pupil's Book p.25

Shared reading

- Read the children the two headlines on pages 38-39 in the anthology, but do not allow them to refer to the text. Ask them to predict what the story is about. Then read the stories together. How close were the predictions? Which of the two headlines gave the best clues?
- What is the main idea of each story? Ask the children to make up a new headline for the duck story, which gives a clearer idea of what the story is about.
- Discuss the pun in the 'What's up duck?' headline.

Focused word/sentence work

- Investigate the use of dashes in the news stories. Newspapers often use these in place of commas. Encourage the children to use commas instead of dashes in their own writing. Remind them that dashes are more acceptable when writing notes.

Independent work

- Children continue their newspaper report, editing their first draft and presenting a final draft.
- Encourage them to check that they have used commas properly in marking the grammatical boundaries in sentences.

Plenary

- Look at the IT texts the children have worked on. Investigate how reading strategies are adapted to the different properties of IT texts, e.g. scrolling. Discuss the editing features they offer: deleting, cutting and pasting, spell checkers, etc.
- Read the finished newspaper reports together. Begin the selection of the best stories for your front page.

DAY 5

Big Book 4A pp.36-39; Pupil's Book p.25

Shared reading

- Discuss how the news stories in the anthology capture the reader's interest.
- Which story is taken from a weekly newspaper? How can the children tell?
- Read the news stories the children have written on days 3 and 4. Make a final selection for the front page. You may choose to have a number of inside pages or different front pages, to allow all the children's work to be used. Discuss how the stories might be edited to fit the space available.
- As preparation for the independent work, ask the children to predict newspaper stories from the evidence of the headlines on page 25 in the pupil's book. All the headlines there are made up. If you prefer you may use actual headlines from newspaper reports you have collected (see 'Preparation' above). The children's reports may then be compared with the original news story.

Focused word/sentence work

- Focus on suitable examples from the children's writing to consolidate key objectives for this term, e.g. grammatical sense and accuracy, use of verbs and adverbs, commas to mark grammatical divisions in sentences, homophones, etc. In an atmosphere of constructive criticism, emphasise good practice as well as the occasional errors.

Independent work

- Children select a headline which interests them, and then make notes to help them write a newspaper style report to go with it.

Plenary

- Review the children's reports based on headlines. Discuss the different ways the headlines have been interpreted.

Consolidation and extension

- Prepare and present your newspaper front page. Display it on a wall for all to read and enjoy.
- Copymaster 9 encourages the children to write a message which might be sent in a bottle.

Homework

- Page 9 in the homework book is set out as a newspaper front page with headlines for the children to write reports. Encourage the children to write a first draft on scrap paper, and then to edit this to fit the space available.

Unit 9

Newspapers

Key Learning Objectives

TL18	To select and examine opening sentences that set scenes, capture interest, etc.; pick out key sentences/phrases that convey information
TL19	To understand and use the terms 'fact' and 'opinion', and distinguish the two
TL20	To identify main features of newspapers
TL21	To predict newspaper stories from the evidence of headlines, making notes, checking against original
TL24	To write newspaper style reports
TL27	To write a non-chronological report, including use of organisational devices
SL2	To investigate verb tenses
SL4	To identify adverbs and understand their functions in sentences
WL8	To spell irregular tense changes

Range:	Newspaper report, article, advertisement, weather forecast
Texts:	'The postman's spat with a black and white cat', *The Express*, 'Houseplants . . .'; 'Weather'; 'For Sale'
Resources:	Big Book 4A pp.40-43 Pupil's Book 4 pp.26-29 Homework Book 4 p.10: Verb tense

DAY 1

Big Book 4A pp.40-41; Pupil's Book pp.26-27

Shared reading

- Read the headline to the children before they see the text. Ask them to predict what the story is about.
- Explore the features of the text: headline, sub-headline, by-line, photographs, captions, columns and paragraphs. How many paragraphs are there?
- How does the report capture the reader's interest? Ask the children to explain the pun in the headline. Discuss the opening sentence. How does it make the reader want to read on?
- What is the main idea of the report?

Focused word/sentence work

- Ask the children to identify two-syllable words with double consonants, e.g. butter, puzzled, happy.
- Identify homophones in the text, e.g. wait (weight), off (of), by (buy), mail (male). Ask the children to use the homophone pairs in sentences to show the different meanings.

Independent work

- Children answer questions about the news report.

Plenary

- Review the children's independent text work. Explain how to use the text to find literal answers, and how to use clues where information is not given directly.

DAY 2

Big Book 4A pp.40-41; Pupil's Book p.27

Shared reading

- Ask the children to retell the story of Snoopy in their own words. Which are the key paragraphs in the text, conveying the main information? (Paragraphs 2 and 4.) What is the function of the other paragraphs? (Introduction, further detail, quotes.)
- Discuss the difference between fact and opinion. Ask the children to read what Mrs Perham has to say, and to identify one fact and one opinion.
- Is it really true that 'the cat has developed a taste for human blood'. Or is simply that she has taken an intense dislike to the postman? Why does the reporter make such a claim?

Focused word/sentence work

- Ask the children to identify nouns in the passage. Make a list. Classify them into common and proper nouns.
- Ask the children to identify the adjectives. Which nouns do they qualify?
- Identify verbs in the passage. Sort them into present and past tense.
- Identify the adverbs. Note that most adverbs end in *-ly*, but there are exceptions, e.g. friendly, family. What kind of words are those?

Independent work

- Children consolidate their understanding of nouns, adjectives, verbs and adverbs by doing the activities on page 27 in the pupil's book.

Plenary

- Review the children's independent work, re-emphasising teaching points and clarifying misconceptions.

DAY 3

Pupil's Book p.28

Shared writing, including focused word/sentence work

- Explain to the children that they are about to plan a report on their own school, as if for a newspaper or magazine. Discuss how such a non-chronological report is different from a report of an event, e.g. present tense, and the use of headings for different aspects of the subject.
- Consider the headings listed on page 28 in the pupil's book. What information might be given under each one?
- Look at the list of questions on page 28 in the pupil's book. Organise them under the appropriate headings.
- Plan the report by making notes, heading by heading. Delete unimportant information. Show how some of the details can be generalised.
- All paragraphs but one will be factual. Which is the exception?

- Discuss ways of capturing the reader's attention, e.g. title, opening sentence, illustrations.
- Discuss how adjectives and adverbs can be used to add colour to the report.

Independent work

- Children begin writing their non-chronological report.

Plenary

- Review the work in progress, offering help and encouragement.

DAY 4

Big Book 4A pp.42-43; Pupil's Book pp.28-29

Shared reading

- What is the purpose of each of the three texts?
- How are the texts similar? How are they different?
- What is the main idea of the article on houseplants?
- Explore how the article on houseplants begins in the third person and continues in the second person as instructions. How does it end?
- Ask the children to explain how to water houseplants correctly.

Focused word/sentence work

- Ask the children to identify the adjectives and adverbs in the houseplants article. Which nouns and verbs do they qualify?
- Ask which adjectives end in *-y*, e.g. many, empty, sunny, cloudy. Ask the children to use these adjectives in sentences of their own.

Independent work

- Children complete their non-chronological report.

Plenary

- Review the children's reports.

DAY 5

Big Book 4A pp.42-43; Pupil's Book p.29

Shared reading

- How is the weather forecast set out? How do you know what the forecast is for your own area? What do the abbreviations mean?
- What do the abbreviations in the advertisement mean?
- What reason does the advertiser give for selling the camcorder? Might there be some other reason? What questions would you need to ask if you were interested in buying?
- What other kinds of information do newspapers give?

Focused word/sentence work

- Ask the children to turn the weather forecast into a past tense report.
- Identify the homophones in the houseplants text, e.g. know (no), of (off), too (to, two), pour (poor), hour (our), see (sea). Ask the children to use them in sentences to show their different meanings.

Independent work

- Children answer questions on the different types of newspaper information.

Plenary

- Review the week's work, consolidating teaching points.

Consolidation and extension

- Publish the children's report on the school. This may be done by using IT to draft and edit the text. Photographs and artwork may be scanned in and positioned within the text. The final version may then be printed out.
- Collect examples of different types of newspaper information. Discuss their content, structure, vocabulary, style, layout and purposes.

Homework

- Page 10 in the homework book consolidates work on verb tense, giving practice in changing present to past tense, including irregular tense changes.

Unit 10 Poems About School

Key Learning Objectives

TL7 To compare and contrast poems on similar themes
TL14 To write poems based on personal or imagined experience linked to poems read
SL2 To investigate verb tenses
WL8 To spell irregular tense changes
WL13 To use a rhyming dictionary

Range:	Poems based on a common theme – school
Texts:	'I Went Back', Gwen Dunn; 'He who owns the whistle rules the world', Roger McGough; 'Out of School', Hal Summers; 'Mr Fitzsimmons', Stanley Cook
Resources:	Big Book 4A pp.44-48 Pupil's Book 4 pp.30-33 Homework Book 4 p.11: The past tense Copymaster 10: Finding rhymes Copymaster 11: Revision – assessment master for term 1

Preparation

- Make a rhyming dictionary available for days 3, 4 and 5, and for copymaster 10.

DAY 1

Big Book 4A pp.44-46; Pupil's Book pp.30-31

Shared reading

- Read the first two poems. What are they about? How are they similar? How are they different?
- Ask the children to explain why nothing was the same for the child returning to school on Monday. Make a list of the things the child had missed. Which do they think was the hardest to bear? Why? Why did the child feel differently on Tuesday?
- 'He who owns the whistle rules the world' gives us the thoughts of the teacher. Ask the children to explain how the sun was playing truant, and how the rain was like scratching fingernails on a blackboard? Why did Roger McGough choose these words? What is unpleasant about the scratching fingernails?
- What is an Acme Thunderer? (A whistle.) How does it bring the world to a standstill?

Focused word/sentence work

- Ask the children to define these words: register, name, puppet, rain, playground, silent, question, answer.
- Ask the children to choose a classroom object and then define it.

Independent work

- Children answer the questions on the poems.

Plenary

- Review the children's independent text work. Discuss their preferences.

DAY 2

Big Book 4A pp.44-46; Pupil's Book p.31

- Which poem do the children like best/least? Why?
- Which lines do they like best? Why?
- What pictures do the poems make in their minds?
- How do the poems make them feel?
- Which poem rhymes? What is its rhyming pattern?

Focused word/sentence work

- Revise work on verbs. Ask the children to identify powerful verbs in the poems, e.g. bloom, dive-bomb, execute.
- Ask the children to change 'He who owns the whistle rules the world' from present to past tense.

Independent work

- Children revise the past tense and explore further irregular tense changes.

Plenary

- Review the children's independent work. Consolidate teaching points, clarifying any misconceptions.

DAY 3

Big Book 4A pp.44-48; Pupil's Book pp.30, 32-33

Shared reading and writing, including focused word/sentence work

- Children read the poems on pages 47-48 in the anthology. Discuss what they are about. Compare and contrast them.
- Children read the earlier poems again. How are they similar to or different from the new ones?
- Discuss ways of using all the poems in this unit as models or inspiration for the children's own.
- Select a poem to use as a model for a shared poem. Brainstorm ideas and make notes. Brainstorm suitable words and phrases and make a list. Choose the best of the ideas and plan how they may be developed in your poem.

Independent work

- Children choose a poem to use as a model and write their own.

Plenary

- Review the work in progress, offering help and encouragement. Read aloud any completed poems.

DAY 4

Big Book 4A pp.47-48; Pupil's Book pp.32-33

Shared reading

- Read the poems on pages 47-48 in the anthology. What are they about? How are they similar? How are they different?
- Consider the form and language of the poems. What pattern do they make on the page? Do they have a strong rhythm? Do they have a regular rhyming pattern?
- Show the children how to use a rhyming dictionary.

Focused word/sentence work

- Identify the rhyming words in the two poems. Ask the children to think of other words which rhyme with them, or to find rhymes in a rhyming dictionary.
- Emphasise that rhyming words do not always have the same spelling pattern.

Independent work

- Children choose a second poem to write, or use a rhyming dictionary to compose jingles.

Plenary

- Ask the children to read aloud their poems and jingles.

DAY 5

Big Book 4A pp.44-48; Pupil's Book p.33

Shared reading

- Ask the children which lines they like best and why.
- Ask them to explain these lines from 'Out of School': 'Aviators wheeling off', 'Mousy ones stealing off', 'Tails of mufflers', 'A kennelful of snarlings'.
- What sounds are described in the poem?
- Compare the effect of the last line, 'All gone home', with other lines in the poem. How is it different? Why?
- Ask the children to choose a poem from those in this unit to read aloud, and to say why they like it.

Focused word/sentence work

- Ask the children to identify the powerful verbs in 'Out of School', e.g. reeling, squealing, wheeling, stealing, thinning. Challenge them to use them in sentences of their own.
- Ask the children to use the rhyming dictionary to find rhymes for words ending in *-ee* or *-ea*.

Independent work

- Children answer questions about the poems 'Mr Fitzsimmons' and 'Out of School'.

Plenary

- Review the week's work, re-emphasising teaching points and clarifying misconceptions.

Consolidation and extension

- Compile the children's poems into a school poems anthology.
- Encourage the children to read the poems aloud to the class and to children in other classes.
- Copymaster 10 encourages the children to collect words which rhyme, perhaps by using a rhyming dictionary. Emphasise to the children that rhyming words do not always have the same spelling pattern.

Homework

- Page 11 in the homework book consolidates work on irregular tense changes.

ASSESSMENT

Copymaster 11 is an assessment master of key word and sentence objectives for term 1, testing definitions, homophones, past tense, adverbs and sentence construction. Indirectly it will also test vocabulary, spelling and handwriting. The completed sheet will be useful as a record of progress, together with examples of the pupil's text work.

HALF-TERMLY PLANNER

Year 4 • Term 2 • Weeks 1–5

SCHOOL ____________ **CLASS** ________ **TEACHER** ____________

		Phonetics, spelling and vocabulary	Grammar and punctuation	Comprehension and composition	Texts
Continuous work Weeks 1–5		WL 1, 2, 3, 4, 8	SL 4		**Range** **Fiction and poetry:** stories/novels about imagined worlds; sci-fi, fantasy adventure; stories in series; modern poetry
Blocked work **Week**	**Unit**				**Titles**
1	11	WL 8	SL 1, 3	TL 1, 2, 4, 5, 10, 13	extracts from *Dragons Live Forever,* Robert Swindells
2	12	WL 9	SL 1	TL 1, 2, 3, 4, 5, 10, 13	extracts from *The Iron Man,* Ted Hughes
3	13	WL 13	SL 1, 3, 4	TL 4, 5, 7, 11	poems: 'The Magician's Attic', Harold Massingham; 'The Bogeyman', Jack Prelutsky; 'In the Wood', Sheila Simmons
4	14	WL 7	SL 1	TL 1, 2, 3, 4, 5, 8, 9, 10, 13	extracts from *Return of the Mummy* and *Night of the Living Dead III,* R. L. Stine
5	15	WL 9,11	—	TL 1, 2, 3, 4, 8, 12	extracts from *The Spaceball,* Maggie Freeman and *The Boy Who Saved Earth,* Jim Slater

Focus on Literacy Teacher's Resource Book 4 © Barry and Anita Scholes, HarperCollins*Publishers* Ltd 1999

HALF-TERMLY PLANNER

Year 4 • Term 2 • Weeks 6–10

SCHOOL ____________________ **CLASS** ________ **TEACHER** ____________

		Phonetics, spelling and vocabulary	Grammar and punctuation	Comprehension and composition	Texts
Continuous work Weeks 6–10		WL 1, 2, 3, 14, 15, 16, 17			**Range** **Fiction and poetry:** stories/novels about imagined worlds; sci-fi, fantasy adventure; stories in series; classic and modern poetry, including poems from different cultures and times **Non-fiction:** information books on same or similar themes; explanation
Blocked work					
Week	**Unit**				**Titles**
6	**16**	WL 5, 10		TL 14, 15, 16, 17, 18, 19, 20, 21, 22, 23, 24, 25	extract from *Coffee*, Rhoda Nottridge; book covers, contents page, index
7	**17**	WL 12		TL 14, 17, 18, 19, 20, 21, 22, 24, 25	extract from *Planet Earth*, Joanne Jessop and *Discovering Worms*, Jennifer Coldrey
8	**18**	WL 6, 12		TL 14, 17, 18, 19, 20, 21, 22, 24, 25	information text: 'More about soil' and poems: 'Rabbit and Lark', James Reeves; 'The Mole', Stanley Cook
9	**19**	WL 10, 11	SL 1, 2	TL 5, 6, 7, 11, 13	poems: 'Full fathom five . . .', William Shakespeare; 'Sea Shell', Enid Madoc-Jones; 'Sea-Fever', John Masefield; 'The Sea', James Reeves; 'Morning', Grace Nichols
10	**20**	WL 12	SL 1, 2	TL 1, 2, 3, 4, 5, 10, 13	extracts from *The Voyage of the Dawn Treader*, C. S. Lewis, Collins and *The Hobbit*, J. R. R. Tolkien, Collins

Unit 11

A Dragon in a Cage

Key Learning Objectives

TL1	To understand how writers create imaginary worlds, and to show how the writer has evoked it through detail
TL2	To understand how settings influence events and incidents in stories and how they affect characters' behaviour
TL4	To understand how the use of expressive and descriptive language can create moods, arouse expectations, build tension and describe emotions
TL 5	To understand the use of figurative language in prose
TL10	To develop use of settings in own writing, making use of work on adjectives and figurative language to describe settings effectively
TL13	To write own examples of descriptive, expressive language based on those read
SL1	To revise work on adjectives from Y3 term 2 and investigate adjectival phrases
SL3	To understand the significance of word order
WL8	To read and spell accurately the words in Appendix List 2

Range:	Fantasy adventure
Texts:	Extracts from *Dragons Live Forever,* Robert Swindells
Resources:	Big Book 4B pp.4-8 Pupil's Book 4 pp.34-36 Homework Book 4 p.12: Spelling – words from Appendix List 2 Copymaster 12: Presentation master for description/story

DAY 1

Big Book 4B pp.4-6; Pupil's Book pp.34-35

Shared reading

- Read the passage aloud. Ask the children to retell the story in their own words.
- Investigate the setting. Is it realistic or fantastic? How can the children tell? Which words and phrases build up pictures of the setting? Ask the children to make notes.
- How is the behaviour of the children in the story affected by the setting? Consider these aspects: they decided to go at night, and so needed to creep out; they tried hard not to be heard; they had to pluck up courage to enter the cellar (the words 'Nikki bit her lip' reveal this); they needed a torch.
- How might Nikki and Sajida have felt at different points in the story?

Focused word/sentence work

- Ask the children to pick out the compound words in the passage, e.g. downstairs, tiptoe, torchlight, flagstones. Explore the words within these words.

Independent work

- Children answer the questions on the story.

Plenary

- Review the children's independent text work. Remind the children how to use the text to find literal answers, and how to use clues where information is not given directly.

DAY 2

Big Book 4B pp.4-6; Pupil's Book p.35

Shared reading

- Focus on the use of expressive and figurative language, e.g. 'Nikki climbed into the throat of the house'. Why is this more effective than saying, 'Nikki climbed into the cellar-chute'? What effect does the use of figurative language have on the mood of the passage and the reader's expectations? Does it make the reader feel less or more excited/anxious?
- What effect do the last two sentences have on the mood of the passage? How do they make the class feel?
- Ask the children to predict what might happen next in the story. Explore different possibilities and consequences.

Focused word/sentence work

- Explore changing the word order in selected sentences. Notice how some re-orderings destroy meaning, e.g. 'They happened but nothing waited'; some make sense but change meanings, e.g. 'Nikki crept downstairs, put on some clothes, and left the house'; others may be re-ordered to retain meaning, e.g. 'Into the throat of the house climbed Nikki'.
- Investigate how commas, connectives and full stops are used in the text to join and separate clauses, e.g. 'Sajida leaned into the chute, holding her wrists'. Ask the children to re-order this sentence to retain meaning. Where does the comma go now?

Independent work

- Children explore changing word order to retain and to change meaning.

Plenary

- Review the children's independent work. Consolidate teaching points, clarifying any misconceptions.

DAY 3

Big Book 4B pp.4-6; Pupil's Book p.36

Shared reading/writing, including focused word/sentence work

- Revise the terms 'adjective' and 'noun'. Ask the children to pick out adjectives from the passage. Which nouns do they describe? Which adjectives do the children find particularly effective? Why?
- Investigate the adjectival ending in 'sickish smell'. How does the ending change the meaning? Encourage the children to suggest other adjectives with that ending.

- Make a list of the words and phrases which give detail about the cellar. Look at the pictures in Unit 11 in the pupil's book. What detail can the children see there? Brainstorm expressive and descriptive words and phrases.
- Consider the remaining four senses. Ask which are appropriate here to describe aspects of the cellar and the dragons.
- Brainstorm words and phrases to describe the feelings of the girls.
- Children choose the best words and phrases from the list to write an exciting description which creates mood, arouses expectations, builds tension and describes emotions.

Independent work

- Children write a description of the cellar setting.

Plenary

- Review the children's descriptions. Praise good use of descriptive, expressive language.

DAY 4

Big Book 4B pp.7-8; Pupil's Book p.36

Shared reading

- Read the second extract from the story on pages 7-8 in the anthology.
- How is this different from the children's predictions on day 2? Might other predictions still work out the way they expected?
- Which words and phrases create the mood, build tension and arouse expectations?
- Consider the figurative language in 'a tongue of flame' and 'firelight danced in their eyes'. Why are these particularly expressive?
- Ask the children to read aloud their own descriptions. Discuss how these may be incorporated into a story which continues where the second extract left off.

Focused word/sentence work

- Ask the children to define these words in no more than four words: cage, grin, free, beast, companion, heap, eat, sound.
- Explore the use of commas in the text.

Independent work

- Children incorporate their descriptions of the setting into a story telling what happens next to the girls and the dragons.

Plenary

- Review the children's stories.

DAY 5

Big Book 4B pp.4-8; Pupil's Book p.36

Shared reading

- Ask the children to retell the complete story with reference to both extracts.
- Ask the children to read aloud their own stories in an atmosphere of constructive criticism.

Focused word/sentence work

- Brainstorm words with the same spelling patterns as b<u>urn</u>, fl<u>ame</u>, b<u>ar</u>, p<u>ush</u>, c<u>age</u>, l<u>ight</u>, c<u>one</u>, etc.
- Explain the difference between an adjective and an adjectival phrase. Find an example in the text, e.g. a flicker <u>of fire</u>. Use words from the text to build adjectival phrases, e.g. a dragon <u>with firelight in its eyes</u>, a cage <u>with bars</u>, a cage <u>of wood</u>.

Independent work

- Children explore adjectives and adjectival phrases.

Plenary

- Review the week's work, re-emphasising teaching points and clarifying misconceptions.

Consolidation and extension

- Ask the children to prepare a final draft of their stories for publication.
- Copymaster 12 is a presentation master for the description or story. It may be completed in the children's best handwriting or used for an IT printout. If using the latter then check that the text fits the blank part of the sheet, without overprinting the border.

Homework

- Page 12 in the homework book helps the children to sort, use and spell words from Appendix List 2.

Unit 12

The Iron Man

Key Learning Objectives

TL1 To understand how writers create imaginary worlds, and to show how the writer has evoked it through detail

TL2 To understand how settings influence events and incidents in stories and how they affect characters' behaviour

TL3 To compare and contrast settings across a range of stories; to evaluate, form and justify preferences

TL4 To understand how the use of expressive and descriptive language can create moods, arouse expectations, build tension, describe attitudes or emotions

TL5 To understand the use of figurative language in prose; locate use of simile

TL10 To develop use of settings in own writing, making use of work on adjectives and figurative language to describe settings effectively

TL13 To write own examples of descriptive, expressive language based on those read. Link to work on adjectives and similes.

SL1 To revise work on adjectives from Y3 term 2 and link to expressive and figurative language in stories and poetry:
- constructing adjectival phrases
- examining comparative and superlative adjectives
- relating adjectives to suffixes which indicate degrees of intensity

WL9 To use alternative words and expressions which are more accurate or interesting than common choices.

Range:	Fantasy story
Texts:	Extracts from *The Iron Man*, Ted Hughes
Resources:	Big Book 4B pp.9-13 Pupil's Book 4 pp.37-39 Homework Book 4 p.13: Synonyms

Preparation

- Make a thesaurus available for days 3 and 4, preferably *Collins Junior Thesaurus*.

DAY 1

Big Book 4B pp.9-11; Pupil's Book pp.37-38

Shared reading

- Read the passage aloud to the children. Investigate the setting. Is it realistic or fantastic? How can the children tell? What aspect of the story is fantastic? Which words and phrases describe the setting? Ask the children to make notes of those words.
- How does the story make the children feel? Which words and phrases create those feelings?
- Ask the children to explain where the Iron Man was approaching from, and why Hogarth could at first see only two green lights.
- Ask the children to retell the story in their own words.

Focused word/sentence work

- Experiment with changing the past tense of the extract into the present tense. Ask the children to imagine they are giving a running commentary on the events in the manner of a radio or TV commentator. Does such a change make the account more, or less, exciting? Why?

Independent work

- Children answer the questions on the story.

Plenary

- Review the children's independent text work. Remind the children how to use the text to find literal answers, and how to use clues where information is not given directly.

DAY 2

Big Book 4B pp.9-11; Pupil's Book p.38

Shared reading

- Compare and contrast the setting of this story with the extract from *Dragons Live Forever* in Unit 11, e.g. indoors and outdoors, an expected danger and an unexpected danger, a place where the children do not belong and the countryside around Hogarth's home. Note that both settings are in semi-darkness. Why is this more dramatic?
- Which setting do the children prefer? Why?
- Investigate the use of expressive and descriptive language in the descriptions of the Iron Man and the farmer.
- Discuss stories with related themes, e.g. where threatening creatures appear, such as monsters, giants, aliens, etc.

Focused word/sentence work

- Draw attention to the comparative adjectival ending of taller. How does it change the meaning of the word 'tall'?
- Discuss the effect on meaning of the suffixes *-ish*, *-er* and *-est*. What affect does the adverb 'very' have when applied to an adjective?
- Compare adjectives on a scale of intensity, e.g. tallish, tall, taller, very tall, tallest.
- Revise adjectival phrases. Ask the children to pick out adjectival phrases from the text, e.g. taller than a house; with green headlamp eyes; with a fat, red-mouthed laugh.
- Encourage the children to construct adjectival phrases of their own, e.g. the farmer with a red face.

Independent work

- Children examine comparative and superlative adjectives and the suffixes which relate to intensity: *-ish, -er, -est.*
- Children construct adjectival phrases.

Plenary

Challenge the children to use the words from their comparative adjectives chart in sentences to show their meaning.

DAY 3

Big Book 4B pp.9-13; Pupil's Book p.39

Shared reading and writing, including focused word/sentence work

- Read the text again. Discuss what might happen next.
- Plan the story of what happens when Hogarth and his father meet the Iron Man, using the 'introduction, build-up, main event, ending' structure as outlined on page 39 in the pupil's book.
- Decide on a setting for the story. If you prefer you may read the second extract on page 12 in the anthology, and use that setting.
- Brainstorm words and phrases which will create moods, arouse expectations, build tension, and describe attitudes and emotions.
- Encourage the children to use a thesaurus to find suitable synonyms, e.g. for 'big' in the description of the Iron Man.
- Plan the story, paragraph by paragraph, outlining plot and noting suitable words and phrases.

Independent work

- Children write their story about the Iron Man.

Plenary

- Review the work in progress, offering help and encouragement.

DAY 4

Big Book 4B pp.9-13; Pupil's Book p.39

Shared reading

- Examine the setting in this further extract: the farmer's yard on a rainy night, and the road home. Which details create mood and arouse expectations? What do the children expect will happen?
- Discuss how the text builds up to the appearance of headlights in the tree.
- Hogarth's father has not yet seen the eyes of the Iron Man and so is unaware of their true nature, but the reader knows. How might this lack of knowledge put his father in danger?
- Discuss how this second appearance of the headlamp eyes creates a different mood and different expectations from that of the first appearance. The first time they appear the headlamps are a mystery, but the author has aroused our expectations of danger by describing the feelings of Hogarth. When the headlamps appear a second time they are no longer a mystery: the reader knows that they are the eyes of the Iron Man. He also knows from the description of the farmer's yard just what the Iron Man is capable of. This is the kind of suspense for which the late film director Alfred Hitchcock is famous. The reader knows more than the character. He knows precisely the danger the character faces, but is unable to warn him. How does that make the reader feel?

Focused word/sentence work

- Explore expressive language in the description of the farmer's yard.
- Ask the children to identify adjectives and adjectival phrases in the text.

Independent work

- Children continue their writing.

Plenary

- Review the children's writing. Choose children to prepare their stories for reading aloud in the plenary session on day 5.

DAY 5

Big Book 4B pp.9-13; Pupil's Book p.39

Shared reading

- Examine the use of paragraphs in the extracts. How many paragraphs are there? What is the main idea of each one?
- How does the author show the thoughts of Hogarth's father?
- What might happen next?

Focused word/sentence work

- Identify the expression 'as fast as he could' in the text. What other expressions can the children think of which begin 'as fast . . . ', 'as quick . . .' or 'as swift . . .'?
- Explain that such expressions are similes: a word picture in which an object is compared to something else.
- Encourage the children to think of other similes, and to use them in sentences to show their meaning.

Independent work

- Children explore similes on page 39 in the pupil's book.

Plenary

Children read aloud their stories.

- Review the week's work, re-emphasising teaching points and clarifying misconceptions.

Consolidation and extension

- Discuss the children's lists of synonyms (see 'Homework' below). Challenge them to show the meaning of selected synonyms by using them in sentences to show their meaning.

Homework

Page 13 in the homework book focuses on synonyms. A thesaurus will be useful, though not essential, for this activity.

Unit 13 Strange Places

Key Learning Objectives

TL4 To understand how the use of expressive and descriptive language can create moods, arouse expectations, build tension, describe attitudes or emotions

TL 5 To understand the use of figurative language in poetry and prose; compare poetic phrasing with narrative/descriptive examples; locate use of simile

TL7 To identify different patterns of rhyme and verse in poetry, and to read these aloud effectively

TL11 To write poetry based on the structure and/or style of poems read

SL1 To revise work on adjectives from Y3 term 2 and link to expressive and figurative language in stories and poetry:

- comparing adjectives on a scale of intensity
- relating adjectives to suffixes which indicate degrees of intensity

SL3 To understand the significance of word order

SL4 To recognise how commas, connectives and full stops are used to join and separate clauses; to identify in their writing where each is more effective

WL13 To investigate a range of suffixes which can be added to nouns and verbs to make adjectives

Range:	Modern poetry
Texts:	'The Magician's Attic', Harold Massingham; 'The Bogeyman', Jack Prelutsky; 'In the Wood', Sheila Simmons
Resources:	Big Book 4B pp.14-17 Pupil's Book 4 pp.40-42 Homework Book 4 p.14: Exploring word order Copymaster 13: Collecting adjectives

DAY 1

Big Book 4B pp.14-15; Pupil's Book p.40-41

Shared reading

- Tell the children to listen carefully as you read the 'The Magician's Attic'. Ask them to picture the scene in their minds. What sights, sounds and smells are described in the poem? Which words and phrases does the poet use? Which descriptions do the children think are the most vivid? Why?
- Read 'The Bogeyman'. Ask what feelings each poem gives. Which details create this response?
- Investigate the patterns of the poems. How are they different? Do the poems rhyme? What is the rhyming scheme? Do the poems have a strong rhythm?

Focused word/sentence work

- Poets often use unusual word order. Investigate examples, e.g. 'In the desolate depths of a perilous place the bogeyman lurks, with a snarl on his face.' Experiment with changing the word order in that sentence. How many different ways of writing it can the children suggest? What effect do these changes have on the meaning, rhyme and rhythm of those lines? Which order works best?
- Discuss the use of commas in the sentence about the bogeyman. Where are commas required when the same sentence is re-ordered?
- Page 14 in the homework book has further work on re-ordering words to retain meaning.

Independent work

- Children answer questions about the poems.

Plenary

- Review the children's independent text work.

DAY 2

Big Book 4B pp.14-15; Pupil's Book pp.40-41

Shared reading

- Read aloud 'The Bogeyman'. How does the poem make the children feel? How is that effect achieved? How is the poem different from 'The Magician's Attic'? Compare their use of expressive language. Which poem do the children prefer? Ask them to justify their preferences.
- Compare the expressive language of 'The Bogeyman' to that in the extracts from *Dragons Live Forever* in Unit 11, and *The Iron Man* in Unit 12. Investigate differences in voice, style and form.

Focused word/sentence work

- Point out the use of commas in a list of adjectives, e.g. 'For this is where he keeps them, old, splintered, broken, worn-out wizard wands.'
- Ask the children to identify the adjectives in the poems. Explore the endings of those made from nouns and verbs, e.g. creaking, cluttered, peaceful, broken, perilous, sunless, steely.
- Discuss other such suffixes, e.g. childlike, heroic, seaworthy.
- Copymaster 13 is designed for the children to collect and record adjectives made from nouns and verbs. Encourage them to find adjectives from their own experience and from their reading.

Independent work

- Children explore a range of suffixes that can be added to nouns and verbs to make adjectives.

Plenary

- Review the children's independent work, re-emphasising teaching points and clarifying misconceptions.

DAY 3

Big Book 4B pp.14-15; Pupil's Book p.42

Shared reading and writing, including focused word/sentence work

- Tell the children that you are going to plan together a poem based on the 'The Magician's Attic'. Read the poem again.
- Identify the similes, e.g. 'musty as the russet smell of old burnt toast and almonds', 'like a toadstool stalk', 'quieter than islands'.
- Look at the suggestions on page 42 in the pupil's book of other mysterious places to write about. Discuss them with the children. Consider the objects that might be found there.
- Choose a setting for the shared writing. Brainstorm ideas for objects, sights, sounds, smells, and flavours. Encourage the children to invent expressive language to describe them. Make a list of their ideas.
- Sort the ideas and select the best ones for your poem. Follow the model as closely as possible, taking into account its vocabulary, patterns of rhyme, similes, etc.

Independent work

- Children use the shared plan for their own poem, or plan and write a poem about a different setting.

Plenary

- Review the work in progress, offering help and encouragement. Praise the use of expressive language. Draw attention to effective adjectival phrases, and to adjectives made from nouns or verbs.

DAY 4

Big Book 4B pp.16-17; Pupil's Book p.42

Shared reading

- Read the poem 'In the Wood'. How is this place different from the setting of the earlier poems in this unit? In what ways is it ordinary? In what ways is it special?
- How does the writer feel about this place? Which words tell you?
- How does the poem make the children feel? Which words create this feeling?
- Explore the use of expressive language, e.g. 'snatching brambles', 'fern-fronds lay long hands over me', 'deep in the ocean of leaves'. Why did the poet choose those words?

Focused word/sentence work

- Ask the children to identify the adjectives in the text. Which ones have been made from nouns or verbs, e.g. snatching, dynamic? Which ones have been made from joining two words together with a hyphen?
- Ask the children to identify an example of an adverbial phrase.

Independent work

- Children continue their writing from day 3.

Plenary

- Review the children's poems. Ask the children to prepare for reading them aloud at a future time.

DAY 5

Big Book 4B pp.14-17; Pupil's Book p.42

Shared reading

- Discuss the way in which the scene described in 'The Wood' gradually becomes more peaceful.
- Explore the pattern of the poem. Are the verses regular? Consider the number of lines and the line length. Does the poem have a strong rhythm? Does it rhyme?
- Compare the poem to the earlier poems in this unit.

Focused word/sentence work

- Select words from the poem for the children to define in four words or less, e.g. wood, track, secret, quiet, ocean, summer.
- Explore how adjectives can be compared on a scale of intensity. Choose words from the passage, e.g. quiet, thin, minute. Brainstorm similar words and sort them in levels of intensity, e.g. microscopic, minute, tiny, small, big, huge, enormous.

Independent work

- Children compare adjectives on a scale of intensity.

Plenary

- Review the children's work on adjectives, discussing their views on scales of intensity.

Consolidation and extension

- Ask the children to prepare and read aloud their favourite of the three poems, or lines they think are particularly effective.
- Ask the children to read aloud their own poems. Compile the poems into an illustrated class anthology.
- Copymaster 13 is for collecting and recording adjectives made from nouns and verbs. Encourage the children to find adjectives from their own experience and from their reading.

Homework

- Page 14 in the homework book explores changing word order. The sentence given can be changed in at least three ways to retain its meaning. Challenge the children to find as many ways as they can of changing the word order in the three sentences, without changing or destroying the meaning.

Unit 14 Inside the Tomb

Key Learning Objectives

TL1 To understand how writers create imaginary worlds, and to show how the writer has evoked it through detail

TL2 To understand how settings influence events and incidents in stories and how they affect characters' behaviour

TL3 To compare and contrast settings across a range of stories; to evaluate, form and justify preferences

TL4 To understand how the use of expressive and descriptive language can create moods, arouse expectations, build tension, describe attitudes or emotions

TL5 To understand the use of figurative language in poetry and prose; compare poetic phrasing with narrative/descriptive examples

TL8 To review a range of stories, identifying authors, themes or treatments

TL9 To recognise how certain types of texts are targeted at particular readers; to identify intended audiences

TL10 To develop use of settings in own writing, making use of work on adjectives and figurative language to describe settings effectively

TL13 To write own examples of descriptive, expressive language based on those read. Link to work on adjectives and similes

SL1 To revise work on adjectives from Y3 term 2 and link to expressive and figurative language in stories and poetry, relating them to adverbs which indicate degrees of intensity; investigating words which can be intensified in these ways and words which cannot

WL7 To recognise and spell the prefixes: *al-*, etc.

Range:	Fantasy adventure story; stories in series – junior horror stories
Texts:	Extracts from *Return of the Mummy*, and *Night of the Living Dead III*, R. L. Stine, from the *Goosebumps* series
Resources:	Big Book 4B pp.18-21 Pupil's Book 4 pp.43-45 Homework Book 4 p.15: Changing past to present tense Copymaster 14: Presentation master for description/story

DAY 1

Big Book 4B pp.18-19; Pupil's Book pp.43-44

Shared reading

- This extract is from a book in the *Goosebumps* series. What kind of books would the children expect this series to feature? For what audience do the children think the series is intended?
- Investigate how the setting is built up from details. Until the line 'The light flickered on' it is described only in the sensations felt by the main character. How does it change from that point?
- How does the passage make the children feel? Which words and phrases create this feeling? At which point did the children feel the full horror of the situation? Which words triggered that feeling? Which words arouse the expectation of further horror to come?
- Explore the way the tension builds by drawing a 'mood thermometer' representing the feelings of the main character. The thermometer rises in blocks, labelled to show the intensity of feeling from worry, through alarm, shock and terror to outright panic. Alongside each block are written the words from the passage which indicate that mood, e.g. worry – 'Weren't they looking for me?; alarm – 'Shaking both arms, I jumped to my feet.', etc. Encourage the children to identify the precise words which trigger those changes.

Focused word/sentence work

- Investigate words which signal place, position and proximity, e.g. down here, on, up, against, in, across, over, from, in mid-air, off, all over, up over, on to the top of, down from, towards. Discuss the way in which these words help to build a picture of the constant movement of the spiders.
- Experiment with changing the past tense of the extract into the present tense. What effect does this have?
- Page 15 in the homework book reproduces part of the extract for transforming into a present tense account.

Independent work

- Children answer the questions about the text.

Plenary

- Review the children's independent text work.

DAY 2

Big Book 4B pp.18-19; Pupil's Book p.44

Shared reading

- How does the behaviour of the main character change as he discovers more and more about where he is?
- Compare the setting of this story with those in Units 11 and 12. Which is the more exciting? Why?
- Identify the use of expressive language and similes in the text, e.g. the wall appeared to move as if alive, the spiders bob and float in mid-air.
- Compare the use of expressive language with the poems in Unit 13. Which is more expressive? Ask the children to justify their answers.

Focused word/sentence work

- Explore adverbs which indicate degrees of intensity when related to adjectives: quite, very, more, less, most, least. Ask the children questions using these adverbs, e.g. at what point in the story did the main character feel quite frightened, very frightened and most frightened? Was he more frightened when he saw the snake than when he saw the spiders? When was he least frightened?

Which part did the children find most exciting? Did they find the end more, or less, exciting than the beginning?

- Experiment with using 'quite', 'very', 'more', 'less', 'most' and 'least' with a range of adjectives. Discuss them on a scale of intensity.
- Identify some adjectives which cannot be intensified in this way, e.g. dead, perfect, better, fatter.

Independent work

- Children explore using the adverbs quite, very, more, less, most and least with adjectives.

Plenary

- Review the children's independent work, re-emphasising teaching points and clarifying misconceptions.

DAY 3

Big Book 4B pp.18-19; Pupil's Book p.45

Shared reading, writing, including focused word/sentence work

- Investigate again how the text creates mood, arouses expectations, builds tension and describes emotions.
- Ask the children to imagine they are in a similar setting such as an underground passage, a room in an old house or castle, or an attic. At first there is no light. What can they hear, smell, touch? What creatures might the darkness be hiding: mice, spiders, beetles, scorpions, snakes? What horrors do they see when the light comes on?
- How do they feel at different parts of the story? What do they want their readers to feel?
- Discuss how to create these moods, arouse expectations, build tension and describe emotions.
- What words and phrases might be used to achieve this? Explore degrees of intensity in adjectives, powerful verbs, similes and other expressive language.
- Plan the writing in four paragraphs.
- Copymaster 14 is a presentation master for the children's final draft.

Independent work

- Children begin their own descriptive writing.

Plenary

- Review the work in progress, offering help and encouragement.

DAY 4

Big Book 4B pp.20-21; Pupil's Book p.45

Shared reading

- Read the extract from the second R. L. Stine book, also in the *Goosebumps* series.
- In what ways are they similar? In what ways are they different?
- Which senses does the author describe? What words does he use?
- What is the effect of the words 'humanly warm'? Why are they put on a line of their own?
- Ask the children to identify the sentences which are not true sentences, i.e. they do not have a verb. Why does the author write in this way?

Focused word/sentence work

- Ask the children to identify the adjectives in the text. Which nouns do they describe?
- Ask the children to define these words in four words or less: darkness, whisper, warm, roof, low, chuckle, sound, strange.

Independent work

- Children continue their writing.

Plenary

- Review the children's writing in an atmosphere of constructive criticism.

DAY 5

Big Book 4B pp.20-21; Pupil's Book p.45

Shared reading

- Explore how the author uses expressive and descriptive language to create the mood, arouse expectations, build tension, and describe emotions.
- Ask the children to identify the words which do this.
- Ask the children to explain how Trina attempts to stay calm. Does the reader expect her to remain calm for long? What makes the children think so?
- What do the children think will happen next?

Focused word/sentence work

- Ask the children to change part or all of the passage into the present tense.
- Discuss the use of the common prefixes *un-, im-, in-,* and *al-*. Ask the children to give examples of words beginning with *un-*, e.g. unafraid, unaware, unlikely, unusual. What effect does *un-* have on a word? Do the same with *im-* and *in-*. What effect do those prefixes have?
- Ask what words can be made from adding *al-* e.g. almost, although, already, altogether, always.

Independent work

- Children work on common prefixes: *un-, im-, in-, al-*.

Plenary

- Review the children's work on prefixes, re-emphasising teaching points and clarifying misconceptions.

Consolidation and extension

- Let the children prepare and read aloud their stories.
- Encourage the children to prepare and read aloud their present tense transformations of the passage on page 15 in the homework book (see below) as a live news report.
- Copymaster 14 is a presentation master for the children's final draft of their description/story.

Homework

- Page 15 in the homework book reproduces part of the extract for transforming into a present tense account.

Unit 15 Goodbye Earth

Key Learning Objectives

TL1	To understand how writers create imaginary worlds, and to show how the writer has evoked it through detail
TL2	To understand how settings influence events and incidents in stories and how they affect characters' behaviour
TL3	To compare and contrast settings across a range of stories; to evaluate, form and justify preferences
TL4	To understand how the use of expressive and descriptive language can create moods, arouse expectations, build tension
TL8	To review a range of stories, identifying treatments
TL12	To collaborate with others to write a story in chapters, using plans with particular audiences in mind
WL9	To use alternative words and expressions which are more accurate or interesting than common choices
WL11	To understand that vocabulary changes over time, through collecting words which have become little used and discussing why

Range:	Story about an imagined world: sci-fi
Texts:	Extract from *The Spaceball*, Maggie Freeman, A & C Black, 1986 Extract from *The Boy Who Saved Earth*, Jim Slater
Resources:	Big Book 4B pp.22-27 Pupil's Book 4 pp.46-48 Homework Book 4 p.16: Description of a space alien Copymaster 15: Collecting words which have become little used

DAY 1

Big Book 4B pp.22-24; Pupil's Book pp.46-47

Shared reading

- Read the extract from *The Spaceball* and discuss the setting. Which features of technology are described? Ask the children to pick out words and phrases which describe them. How can we tell this is a science-fiction story?
- How does the situation affect Cecil's behaviour? What effect does the appearance of the alien have on him? Ask the children to justify their answers.
- Investigate the use of expressive language. Ask what senses the writer describes, e.g. sight, sound, touch. Discuss the description of the alien. Does it give us a clear picture? Is it intended to frighten the reader? Ask the children to give reasons for their answers.

Focused word/sentence work

- Collect and discuss the use of adjectives in the story. Ask the children to classify them.
- Explore the importance of adjectives and adjectival phrases by experimenting with deletions and substitutions. Which synonyms might be substituted? To what extent is the meaning affected?
- Which adjective has the prefix *in-* (invisible)? Which adjectives have the suffixes *-ed, -er, -ible*? Which of these are made from nouns or verbs?

Independent work

- Children answer questions on the extract.

Plenary

- Review the children's independent text work.

DAY 2

Big Book 4B pp.22-24; Pupil's Book p.47

Shared reading

- Compare the situation in this extract with the one in Unit 14 (*Return of the Mummy*). Is Cecil in as great immediate danger as Gabe? How might his danger be potentially even greater? Does the class think the writer intends to frighten the reader in the same way R. L. Stine did? What makes them think so?
- Ask the children to retell the story in their own words.
- What do they think will happen next? Page 47 in the pupil's book has a cloze passage which continues the extract from the point it left off. Make sure that the children appreciate that any word which fits the sense of the passage is allowed. The actual words used by the author are given here for reference purposes only: studied, tiny, right, through, Earth, shiny, long, because, Follow, meet, they, creatures, very, that, off.

Focused word/sentence work

- Experiment with changing the past tense of the extract into the present tense.
- Cecil says, 'I got in by accident'. What else might he have said? Discuss alternative more interesting, descriptive and accurate words he might have used.
- Ask the children to define words from the text in four words or less, e.g. warm, soft, creature, surprise, home.

Independent work

- Children work on the cloze passage.

Plenary

- Review the children's cloze work. How many different, but acceptable words did the children think of? Compare these with those of the author. Why do the children think she chose her words rather than alternative ones? Aim for an appreciation that all writing involves a choice of words, and it is the writer who decides which words are best for his/her purpose and audience.

DAY 3

Big Book 4B pp.22-24; Pupil's Book p.48

Shared writing, including focused word/sentence work

- Page 48 in the pupil's book has ideas to help the children plan a story in chapters. This involves joint planning of the story structure, chapter by chapter, but independent writing of individual chapters.
- First discuss what kind of adventure story the children would like to write, e.g. sci-fi, horror, fantasy. Then ask them to select an audience. Consider the need not to frighten a younger audience.
- The story will need detailed planning, chapter by chapter, so that each writer knows what happens before and after his own chapter. The story plan should be displayed prominently for reference, together with a list of authors.
- Each chapter should then be planned in three or four paragraphs. It may be written by a single child or in pairs, perhaps teaming children of different abilities.
- Encourage revision of the writing.
- Select a small editorial team to check that the story flows consistently between chapters without sudden changes in plot, character or setting. Any such changes will require rewriting individual chapters. Make sure the children understand why this is necessary.
- Collate the chapters and publish the story as a book, with front cover illustrations, back cover 'blurb', a list of chapter titles and authors, illustrations, etc.
- This activity will take a number of sessions and may be continued outside the literacy hour, perhaps as homework.

Independent work

- Children plan their writing.

Plenary

- Review the work in progress, offering help and encouragement.

DAY 4

Big Book 4B pp.25-27; Pupil's Book p.48

Shared reading

- Which detail tells us that this is a sci-fi story?
- What expectations do the children have about the story? What makes them think so?
- How does Marcou know that the danger is worse than his uncle admits?
- What do they think a purple alert is? Is this the most serious alert? How can we tell from the passage?
- What do the numbers 257 and 300 probably mean?

Focused word/sentence work

- Discuss the sci-fi technical vocabulary, e.g. 'visual address unit', 'purple alert', 'communications system', 'propulsion unit'. What might these things be? What more familiar vocabulary might we use?
- Discuss words from the past which are little used today because of changes in fashion and technology, e.g. frock, record-player, cooper, wireless, etc.
- Copymaster 15 is a collection sheet for words which have become little used.
- Investigate the use of commas, connectives and full stops in the text. Notice how clauses are joined and separated.

Independent work

- Children continue working on their story.

Plenary

- Review the children's writing.

DAY 5

Big Book 4B pp.22-27; Pupil's Book p.48

Shared reading

- How is tension built up in this extract?
- Compare this extract with the earlier one in this unit. How is it similar? How is it different? Which is the more serious treatment?
- Is it written for the same audience? What makes the children think so? Which extract do the children prefer? Why?
- Ask the children to read the extract aloud with appropriate intonation and taking account of punctuation.

Focused word/sentence work

- Ask the children to identify an adjective with the prefix *un-*. What effect does this prefix have on the word *usual?*
- Ask what other expression in the passage means to get up (rose). Discuss the overuse of the word *got.*
- Ask the children to suggest alternative words for *got, good* and *nice* in a variety of contexts.

Independent work

- Children explore alternative words for *nice* and *good.*

Plenary

- Review the week's work, consolidating teaching points.

Consolidation and extension

- Publish the children's own story book for others to read.
- Let the children prepare and read aloud their descriptions of space aliens. See below.
- Copymaster 15 is a collection sheet for words which have become little used.

Homework

- Page 16 in the homework book encourages the children to write their own description of a space alien.

Unit 16

Information

Key Learning Objectives

TL14 To practise notemaking: to edit down a sentence or passage by deleting the less important elements, and discuss reasons for editorial choices

TL15 To appraise a non-fiction book for its content and usefulness by scanning

TL16 To prepare for factual research by reviewing what is known, what is needed, what is available and where one might search

TL17 To scan texts in print or on screen to locate key words or phrases, useful headings and key sentences and to use these as a tool for summarising text

TL18 To mark extracts by annotating and by selecting key headings, words or sentences, or alternatively, noting these

TL19 To identify how and why paragraphs are used to organise and sequence information

TL20 To identify from the examples the key features of explanatory texts: purpose, structure, language features, presentation

TL21 To make short notes

TL22 To fill out brief notes into connected prose

TL23 To collect information from a variety of sources and present in one simple format

TL24 To improve the cohesion of written explanations through paragraphing, the use of link phrases and organisational devices

TL25 To write explanations of a process, using conventions identified through reading

WL5 To investigate what happens to words ending in *f* when suffixes are added

WL10 To explore and discuss the implications of words which imply gender, including the *-ess* suffix

Range:	Information books on same or similar theme; explanation
Texts:	Extract from *Coffee*, Rhoda Nottridge; book covers; contents page; index
Resources:	Big Book 4B pp.28-31 Pupil's Book 4 pp.49-51 Homework Book 4 p.17: Plurals ending in *f*; male and female Copymaster 16: Finding out – planning Copymaster 17: Finding out – finding and recording information

Preparation

- Provide information books for the children to practise appraising their content and usefulness by scanning.
- Provide information books, and/or IT sources, on elephants, lions, hippopotamuses, tigers, alligators, camels, kangaroos, ostriches, wolves, pandas, penguins and gorillas or other animals if you prefer.
- Information on how tea is grown and processed will be required for day 5.
- The research and writing activities in this unit are intended for days 3, 4 and 5.

DAY 1

Big Book 4B pp.28-29; Pupil's Book pp.49-50

Shared reading

- Identify the key features and purpose of the explanatory text. Ask how it is structured, e.g. introduction, sequential explanation organised in paragraphs. Ask what language features it has, e.g. present tense, third person, passive voice, connectives of time (first, then). Ask how it is presented, e.g. highlighted words, use of diagram.
- Ask the children to identify the main idea of each paragraph. Why is the text organised in this way?
- What is the purpose of the diagram? Does it make things clearer? How does it show the differences in the manufacture of ordinary and freeze-dried coffee?

Focused word/sentence work

- Ask the children to identify the use of commas in the text. What is their function?
- Discuss why four of the words are highlighted. Ask the children to define these words.

Independent work

- Children answer the questions on the text.

Plenary

- Review the children's independent text work.

DAY 2

Big Book 4B pp.28-29; Pupil's Book p.50

Shared reading

- Ask the children to tell in their own words how instant coffee is made, emphasising the differences between ordinary and freeze-dried coffee.
- Show the children how to make notes by editing down the text, e.g. by deleting the less important words.
- Discuss ways of filling out these notes into connected prose.
- To what extent is the diagram a summary of the text? What doesn't it tell us? Does it tell us anything the text does not?

Focused word/sentence work

- Ask the children to identify the adjectives. Ask which have been made from verbs, e.g. frozen, dried.
- Experiment with changing the word order in selected sentences, e.g. the first two sentences. These are easily re-ordered to retain meaning. How and why will the position of the comma change in the second sentence?

Independent work

- Children make notes on the text, and use them to reconstruct connected prose.

Plenary

- Review the children's notes.

DAY 3

Big Book 4B p.30; Pupil's Book p.51

Shared reading/writing

- Ask the children to look at the book covers on page 30 in the anthology, and predict what they could expect each book to tell them. Encourage them to suggest which great inventions, pets, etc. might be featured in the books. How might the children check to see if the book really does tell about the subjects they suggested?
- Ask the children from which books might we learn about dogs e.g. 'Pets', 'Farm Animals'. Which is likely to be more useful? Why? Ask from which books might we learn about the action of rain on rocks and soil, e.g. Weather, Soil. Which is likely to be more useful? Why?
- Page 51 in the pupil's book has a simple chart about animals for the children to complete using a variety of reference sources. Use copymasters 16 and 17 to help.
- Copymaster 16 is a planning sheet to help the children prepare for reading information books. Discuss with the children the importance of asking themselves what they know about the subject already. This will help them to frame more precisely the questions to be answered. Talk about how they can find information. Discuss the range of sources of information available to them: books in class and school libraries, encyclopedias, IT sources, etc.
- Copymaster 17 is for finding and recording the information they need. Emphasise the importance of writing down the question they need answering – it is all too easy to forget such a question when confronted with lots of information. Show the children how to pick out the key words in the question. Encourage them to narrow down their search by selecting two books, which, from their covers, contents page, etc., seem most likely to help. Ask them to write down the titles of those books in the appropriate space on their recording sheet. The next stage is to copy down the key words from their question and to look these up in the index, noting all relevant page numbers as they do so. This list may then be used to search for the information they need. This process should be repeated with the second book. They may now have the answer to their question, and if so should write it at the foot of their sheet. If not, then they may need a third or fourth book, or an alternative reference source, such as a computer database.

Focused word/sentence work

- Revise alphabetical order to the fourth letter.

Independent work

- Children begin their factual research.

Plenary

- Review the work in progress.

DAY 4

Big Book 4B p.31; Pupil's Book p.51

Shared reading

- Look at the contents page shown on page 31. From which of the books does the class think the contents page comes? Why? Discuss the layout of the contents page. What information does it tell us? What information does it not give? How might we find the precise page where we could learn about hamsters, for example?
- From which book does the class think the index page comes? Why? Discuss the advantages of an index over a contents page when matching page number to subject. Ask what a contents page tells us that an index does not, e.g. the structure and content of the book.

Focused word/sentence work

- Ask the children to define a contents page and an index.
- Investigate the words in the index list. What kind of words are they? Which of those nouns are not plural. Can they be made plural?

Independent work

- Children continue their factual research.

Plenary

- Review the results of the children's research.

DAY 5

Pupil's Book p.51

Shared reading

- Investigate the information books the children are using. Appraise their usefulness by scanning their titles, covers, contents pages, indexes, illustrations, headings, etc.
- Appraise the indexes. How useful are they? Do they give enough information? How easy are they to use?
- Look at the contents pages. What do they tell us about the structure of the books?
- Investigate any encyclopedias the children are using. How are they organised? How easy is it to find the information the children are looking for? Does the encyclopedia have its own index?

Focused word/sentence work

- Investigate what happens to words ending in *f* when a suffix is added, e.g. wolf – wolves.
- Explore and discuss the implications of words which imply gender, including the *ess* suffix, e.g. lion/lioness, king/queen.
- Page 17 in the homework book consolidates this work.

Independent work

- Children continue their factual research on animals.

Plenary

- Review the whole process of finding information.
- Let the children explain how they followed this process in completing their animal charts.

Consolidation and extension

- Display the children's research on animals as a wall chart and discuss their work.

Homework

- Page 17 in the homework book practises on pluralising words ending in f, and gender words.

Unit 17 Soil

Key Learning Objectives

TL14 To practise notemaking: to edit down a sentence or passage by deleting the less important elements, and discuss reasons for editorial choices

TL17 To scan texts in print or on screen to locate key words or phrases, useful headings and key sentences and to use these as a tool for summarising text

TL18 To mark extracts by annotating and by selecting key headings, words or sentences, or alternatively, noting these

TL19 To identify how and why paragraphs are used to organise and sequence information

TL20 To identify from the examples the key features of explanatory texts: purpose, structure, language features, presentation

TL21 To make short notes

TL22 To fill out brief notes into connected prose

TL24 To improve the cohesion of written explanations through paragraphing, the use of link phrases and organisational devices

TL25 To write explanations of a process, using conventions identified through reading

WL12 To define familiar words but within varying constraints

Range:	Information books on same or similar theme; explanation
Texts:	Extract from *Planet Earth*, Joanne Jessop Extract from *Discovering Worms*, Jennifer Coldrey
Resources:	Big Book 4B pp.32-35 Pupil's Book 4 pp.52-55 Homework Book 4 p.18: Definitions

DAY 1

Big Book 4B pp.32-33; Pupil's Book pp.52-53

Shared reading

- Ask the children to look at the layout of the text and to suggest what they expect it to tell them. Which clues helped them decide, e.g. the heading, the illustration? Some children may unconsciously have used 'skimming': reading the text quickly to get an overall impression. Others may have 'scanned', looking for important words. Teach the technique of scanning to the children. Give practice in this by asking them to find the words listed in question 1.
- Discuss the importance of identifying key words in questions when scanning for those words in the text. Explain that once the key word is found in the text it is necessary to read that part of the text carefully to find the answer to the question. Suggest that the children remember these words: Scan, Locate, Read carefully.

Focused word/sentence work

- Make a list of the technical words used in the passage, e.g. 'organic matter', 'logging', 'bacteria', etc. Ask the children to define these words, first by inference from the text and then checking using a dictionary. Use the definitions to make a glossary.

Independent work

- Children practise scanning. The key words are underlined in each question to help the children. Remind them to use detailed reading when they have located those key words in the text.

Plenary

- Review the children's independent text work.

DAY 2

Big Book 4B pp.32-33; Pupil's Book p.53

Shared reading

- What is the purpose of the text?
- How is it structured?
- Discuss the language features. The past tense is used when explaining how soil was formed in the past, and the present tense for how it is continually being enriched. Investigate connectives of time: e.g. when, gradually, over millions of years.
- How is the text presented? How does the illustration support the text?

Focused word/sentence work

- Point out the suffix *-ic* in the word organic. How many words with the same suffix can the children think of?
- Focus on the word 'plough' in the sentence 'Earthworms are like tiny ploughs.' How many other words can the class think of with the letters *ough*? Ask how many different sounds these letters represent, e.g. rough, bough, cough, etc.
- Introduce the children to the cloze passage on page 53 in the pupil's book.

Independent work

- Children work on the cloze passage.

Plenary

- Review the children's cloze work. Any word which fits the sense and grammar of the text is acceptable. The actual words used by the author are given here for reference purposes only: living, man, your, the, different, things, to, with, many, the, garden, planted, from, flowers, insects.

DAY 3

Big Book 4B pp.32-33; Pupil's Book p.54

Shared reading and writing

- What is the main idea of each paragraph of the 'Soil' text in the anthology? Ask the children to pick out the detail which supports each main idea.
- List these details under an appropriate heading for the main idea. Point out that this is an alternative way to make notes.
- Ask the children to identify the key sentences in the text.
- Cover each of the three bulleted points above for the text on page 54 in the pupil's book: 'Attracting moths'.
- Discuss ways of making notes and using them to write a new version of the text, using the structure given.

Independent work

- Children practise writing notes by picking out the key words, and then use these to create connected text.

Plenary

- Ask the children to compare the text they have recreated from their notes to the original text. The layout will be different, but have they included all the important points?

DAY 4

Big Book 4B pp.34-35; Pupil's Book pp.54-55

Shared reading

- Read the text on earthworms. This text is also reproduced on page 55 in the pupil's book.
- What is the purpose of the text? How is it structured?
- Discuss the language features: present tense, use of connectives, e.g. when, also, then.
- How is the text presented? How does the illustration support the text?
- What is the main idea of each paragraph? Ask the children to identify the supporting detail.

Focused word/sentence work

- Investigate the use of commas in the text, e.g. for separating items in a list ('soft, rich, undisturbed ground') and separating clauses.
- Identify the adjectives. Ask the children to use these in sentences of their own.

Independent work

- Children continue their work from day 3 or make notes on the earthworms text and use them to create a connected text, using the structure given.

Plenary

- Review the children's work, re-emphasising teaching points and clarifying misconceptions.

DAY 5

Big Book 4B pp.34-35; Pupil's Book p.55

Shared reading

- Ask the children to explain these processes in their own words: how worms burrow into the soil, how they make worm casts, and why worms are very useful in the soil.
- Practise scanning for keywords in the text, e.g. burrows, casts, ploughs, grasslands, snout, lawn, hot weather, danger, etc.

Focused word/sentence work

- Experiment with changing word order in selected sentences. Discuss words which have to be added or deleted to retain meaning. Which changes destroy meaning? Which result in changing the meaning? Discuss how subsequent words are governed by preceding ones.
- Ask the children to define words from the text in four words or less, e.g. snout, fine, pieces, tiny.

Independent work

- Children scan for key words in the text in order to answer questions. The key words are underlined in the questions in section A, but the children are asked to pick them out for themselves in the section B questions.

Plenary

- Review the week's work, consolidating teaching points.

Consolidation and extension

- Ask the children make up their own questions about the texts for others to answer. Remind them to identify the key words in the questions before they begin to scan for the answers.
- Display and discuss the children's notes, together with the texts they have constructed from them.
- Ask the children to use reference books to find out more about creatures which live in soil, in gardens, etc.

Homework

- Page 18 in the homework book gives practice in making concise definitions.

Unit 18 More About Soil

Key Learning Objectives

TL14 To practise notemaking: to edit down a sentence or passage by deleting the less important elements, and discuss reasons for editorial choices

TL17 To scan texts in print or on screen to locate key words or phrases, useful headings and key sentences and to use these as a tool for summarising text

TL18 To mark extracts by annotating and by selecting key headings, words or sentences, or alternatively, noting these

TL19 To identify how and why paragraphs are used to organise and sequence information

TL20 To identify from the examples the key features of explanatory texts: purpose, structure, language features, presentation

TL21 To make short notes

TL22 To fill out brief notes into connected prose

TL24 To improve the cohesion of written explanations through paragraphing, the use of link phrases and organisational devices

TL25 To write explanations of a process, using conventions identified through reading

WL6 To spell words with the common endings: *-ight*, etc

WL12 To define familiar words but within varying constraints

Range:	Information book on same or similar themes; explanation Modern poetry
Texts:	Information text: 'More about soil' 'Rabbit and Lark', James Reeves 'The Mole', Stanley Cook
Resources:	Big Book 4B pp.36-39 Pupil's Book 4 pp.56-58 Homework Book 4 p.19: Spelling – words with common endings

Preparation

- NB: the writing activities take place on days 2 and 3 in this unit.

DAY 1

Big Book 4B pp.36-37; Pupil's Book pp.56-57

Shared reading

- Ask the children to look at the layout of the text and to suggest what they expect it to tell them. Then ask them what clues the headings give. Explain that this kind of reading is 'skimming' – reading quickly to get an overall impression of what the text is about.
- Look at the questions. Remind the class of the importance of identifying the key words when scanning, and that once the key word is found in the text it is necessary to read that part of the text carefully to find the answer to the question. Reinforce the strategy of 'Scan, Locate, Read carefully'. Ask the children to find the answers to the questions.

Focused word/sentence work

- Ask the children to identify the adverbs which indicate degrees of intensity, e.g. more fertile, many more creatures.
- Experiment with sentences using the words *more, many more* and *truly*.

Independent work

- Children scan for key words in the text to answer questions.

Plenary

- Review the children's independent text work.

DAY 2

Big Book 4B pp.36-37; Pupil's Book pp.56-57

Shared reading/writing

- NB: the writing activities take place on days 2 and 3 in this unit.
- Read the text on soil again. What is its purpose? How is it structured?
- Read the passage for detail, considering each paragraph and its heading in turn. What is the main idea of each paragraph? Does the heading sum up the main idea? What is the main idea of the entire passage? Does its title sum it up? Can the children think of an alternative title for the passage?
- Ask the children to identify the key words and key sentences in the passage.
- Make notes on the first paragraph together. Without referring to the passage, create a connected text using the notes.

Focused word/sentence work

- Ask the children to identify the adjectives in the text. Ask which have been made from verbs, e.g. broken, healthy. Which suffixes have been used to make them?
- Experiment with substituting alternative adjectives. What is their effect on meaning?

Independent work

- Children write their own notes on the text and use the headings to create a connected text from them.

Plenary

- Compare the children's own text with the original passage. Have they left out anything important? How can their text be improved? Is the handwriting sufficiently clear and neat?

DAY 3

Big Book 4B pp.36-37; Pupil's Book pp.56-57

Shared reading

- Discuss the language features of the text. Which tense is used? Ask the children to identify the connectives.
- How is the text presented? How does the illustration support the text?
- Compare this text with the text on soil in Unit 17. How are they similar? How are they different?
- Ask the children to suggest captions for the cycle diagram.

Focused word/sentence work

- Experiment with changing the word order in selected sentences, e.g. the two sentences in paragraph one. How can each sentence be re-ordered to retain meaning? Are additional words necessary to do this? Which changes destroy meaning? Why is this?
- Ask the children to suggest definitions for soil, fertility, nutrients and humus, referring to the passage to help them.

Independent work

- Children copy the cycle diagram, adding their own captions.

Plenary

- Review the children's diagrams and captions. Does the diagram explain the plant-soil cycle clearly enough? How might it be improved?

DAY 4

Big Book 4B pp.38-39; Pupil's Book p.58

Shared reading

- Ask the children to explain why the rabbit and the lark have such different opinions.
- Why do they meet on top of the hill?
- What are the patterns of rhyme and verse in this poem?
- What does the word 'asunder' mean? The word is not used in everyday speech, but is sometimes found in poems, especially older ones.
- What are the patterns of rhyme and verse in 'The Mole'? Compare the poem with 'Rabbit and Lark'.

Focused word/sentence work

- Ask the children to identify the adjectives. Experiment with substitutions. What effect does this have on meaning?
- Ask the children to define common words in the poems, e.g. sunny, high, dark, friends. Encourage them to use as few words as possible.

Independent work

- Children make up their own definitions of everyday words, first in four words, then three, two and one.

Plenary

- Review the children's definitions. Are they clear and accurate?

DAY 5

Big Book 4B pp.38-39; Pupil's Book p.58

Shared reading

- Ask the children to explain why the tunnels mean freedom to the mole.
- What might Stanley Cook be referring to when he calls the mole tube-dweller and talks about the main lines of the underground?
- Why could the mole not tell the difference between darkness and light?
- Which poem do the children prefer? Why?
- Ask the children to read the poems aloud.

Focused word/sentence work

- Investigate words from the poems with common endings, e.g. -ight, -ark, -ill.
- Make a list of words with these endings.
- Encourage the children to use them in sentences of their own.

Independent work

- Children explore the spelling of words with common endings: *-ight*, *-ice*, *-ong* and *-ace*.

Plenary

- Review the children's work on spelling. Ask them to check their spellings with a dictionary and then to learn them.

Consolidation and extension

- Discuss different spelling strategies for learning the spellings from day 5 and from the homework book activities.

Homework

- Page 19 in the homework book explores the spelling of words with common endings: *-ack*, *-ock* and *-tch*.

Unit 19

Full Fathom Five

Key Learning Objectives

TL 5	To understand the use of figurative language in poetry and prose; compare poetic phrasing with narrative/descriptive examples; locate use of simile
TL6	To identify clues which suggest poems are older
TL7	To identify different patterns of rhyme and verse in poetry, and to read these aloud effectively
TL11	To write poetry based on the structure and/or style of poems read
TL13	To write own examples of descriptive, expressive language
SL1	To revise work on adjectives from Y3 term 2, linking to expressive and figurative language in stories and poetry
SL2	To use the apostrophe accurately to mark possession
WL10	To explore and discuss the implications of words which imply gender, including the *-ess* suffix
WL11	To understand that vocabulary changes over time, through collecting words which have become little used and discussing why

Range:	Classic and modern poetry
Texts:	'Full fathom five . . .', William Shakespeare; 'Sea Shell', Enid Madoc-Jones; 'Sea-Fever', John Masefield; 'The Sea', James Reeves
Resources:	Big Book 4B pp.40-43 Pupil's Book 4 pp.59-61 Homework Book 4 p.20: The apostrophe: belonging to Copymaster 18: Presentation master for poem Copymaster 19: Descriptive writing

DAY 1

Big Book 4B pp.40-43; Pupil's Book pp.59-60

Shared reading

- Read each poem in turn. For each one ask the children what it is about, and what feeling it gives them. What pictures does it make in their minds? Which words and phrases make these pictures vivid? Which lines in the poem do the children like best? Why?
- Which clues suggest that 'Full fathom five . . .' and 'Sea-Fever' are older poems? Investigate use of language, vocabulary and archaic words. Why are some of these words little used now?
- Encourage the children to use context clues to guess the meaning of the more difficult words.

Focused word/sentence work

- Ask the class to collect words new to them in the poems, and to check meanings by inference from the surrounding text. Check the precise meanings by using a dictionary.

Independent work

- Children answer the questions on the poems.

Plenary

- Review the children's independent text work.

DAY 2

Big Book 4B pp.40-43; Pupil's Book p.60

Shared reading

- Explore the use of figurative and expressive language in the poems, e.g. adjectives, alliteration, similes.
- Compare this use of language with prose extracts and poems from earlier units.
- Discuss the different patterns of rhyme and verse. Which poem has rhyming couplets? Which has a less regular rhyme pattern? Which does not have a rhyming pattern?
- Read the poems aloud and ask the children to listen to the sound of the words.
- Which poem do the children like best? Ask them to justify their preferences.
- Ask the children to prepare and read out loud their favourite poem.

Focused word/sentence work

- Investigate the use of the apostrophe in 'Sea-Fever'. Ask which examples show possession, e.g. 'the wheel's kick', 'the wind's song', 'the white sail's shaking'. Ask which show contraction, e.g. 'the wind's like a whetted knife'.
- Explain to the class the basic rule for apostrophising singular nouns, e.g. the boy's bike.
- Ask the children to suggest further examples.
- The use of the apostrophe with plural and irregular nouns will be explored on day 5.

Independent work

- Children practise and consolidate their understanding of the apostrophe to denote possession.

Plenary

- Review the children's independent work, re-emphasising teaching points and clarifying misconceptions.

DAY 3

Pupil's Book p.61

Shared reading/writing, including focused word/sentence work

- Read the list poem 'Morning' by Grace Nichols on page 61 in the pupil's book. Discuss ways in which it might be used as a model for a shared poem, using one or more of the ideas given.
- Make a list of the sounds which might be heard, each verb ending in *-ing* as in Grace Nichols' poem.
- Consider the effect of adding an adverb to each verb, so that each line ends in *-ly*.

Independent work

- Children write their own poem.

Plenary

- Ask the children to read their poems out to the class, in an atmosphere of constructive criticism.

DAY 4

Big Book 4B p.41; Pupil's Book p.61

Shared reading/writing, including focused word/sentence work

- Read the poem 'Sea Shell' again.
- Use it as a model for a shared poem. Encourage the children to brainstorm things they might see and hear when holding the shell to their ear. Make a list of their suggestions.
- Brainstorm expressive words and phrases to make vivid pictures of the things on your list. Encourage the children to use figurative language such as similes.
- Discuss the effect of different adjectives, adverbs, etc.

Independent work

- Children write their own poem, or continue the shared poem.
- Copymaster 18 is a presentation master for the children's final draft.

Plenary

- Ask the children to read aloud their own poems.

DAY 5

Big Book 4B pp.40-43; Pupil's Book p.61

Shared reading

- Read 'The Sea' by James Reeves. The poem is an extended metaphor. Explore each verse in turn, discussing the different ways in which the sea is like a dog.
- How is the sound of the sea like a dog in verse one?
- How is the sea like a dog shaking its wet sides in verse two?
- How does the sea change on quiet days?
- Which lines do the children like best? Why?
- What is the pattern of rhyme and verse? Is it regular?
- Ask the children to read the poem aloud.

Focused word/sentence work

- Revise the use of the apostrophe to denote possession with singular nouns. Explain the rules for plural and irregular plural nouns, e.g. boys' shoes, men's hat, children's laughter.
- Give the children practice in using the apostrophe with plural nouns. Suggest plural nouns for them to use in sentences, e.g. ladies – The ladies' hats were blue.

Independent work

- Children practise using the apostrophe to denote possession with singular, plural and irregular plural nouns.

Plenary

- Review the week's work, re-emphasising teaching points and clarifying misconceptions.

Consolidation and extension

- Collect the children's poems into a class anthology.
- Copymaster 18 is a presentation master for the children's sea-shell poems.
- Copymaster 19 has pictures to stimulate the children to write descriptions using expressive language. Discuss the pictures with the children and encourage them to think of suitable descriptive words and phrases.

Homework

- Page 20 in the homework book gives further practice in using the apostrophe to denote possession.

Unit 20

The Unknown Valley

Key Learning Objectives

TL1 To understand how writers create imaginary worlds, and to show how the writer has evoked it through detail

TL2 To understand how settings influence events and incidents in stories and how they affect characters' behaviour

TL3 To compare and contrast settings across a range of stories; to evaluate, form and justify preferences

TL4 To understand how the use of expressive and descriptive language can create moods, arouse expectations, build tension, describe attitudes or emotions

TL5 To understand the use of figurative language in poetry and prose; compare poetic phrasing with narrative/descriptive examples; locate use of simile

TL10 To develop use of settings in own writing, making use of work on adjectives and figurative language to describe settings effectively

TL13 To write own examples of descriptive, expressive language based on those read. Link to work on adjectives and similes

SL1 To revise work on adjectives from Y3 term 2 and link to expressive and figurative language in stories and poetry

SL2 To use the apostrophe accurately to mark possession

WL12 To define familiar words but within varying constraints

Range:	Novel about imagined world: fantasy adventure; stories in series
Texts:	Extracts from *The Voyage of the Dawn Treader*, C. S. Lewis, Collins Extracts from *The Hobbit*, J. R. R. Tolkien, Collins
Resources:	Big Book 4B pp.44-48 Pupil's Book 4 pp.62-64 Homework Book 4 p.21: Proofreading Copymaster 20: Revision – assessment

DAY 1

Big Book 4B pp.44-46; Pupil's Book pp.62-63

Shared reading

- The extract in the anthology is one of C. S. Lewis's *Narnia* books, the magical land that was first entered through a wardrobe in *The Lion, the Witch and the Wardrobe*. In *The Voyage of the Dawn Treader* they gain access when a picture comes to life. Ask the children if they have read any other *Narnia* books, or seen adaptations on television. Explain what a sequel is.
- Discuss the words and phrases which describe the setting. Does it seem a pleasant place? What might the black burnt patches be? Ask the children to justify their answers.
- Make a list of examples of expressive and descriptive language used in the passage, e.g. 'grim peaks and horns of mountains peered over the valley's edge'. What effect do such expressions have? Compare and contrast these with the expressive language used in the poems in Unit 19.
- Ask the class why Eustace shuddered when he looked for a way out of the valley. Which words and phrases describe how he felt and behaved?

Focused word/sentence work

- Refer the children to the list of descriptive language you compiled, and focus on adjectives. Ask the children to find synonymous words for them.
- Consider the effect of the word 'dead' in 'It froze him dead still'. Which other words indicating degrees of intensity might used instead, e.g. quite, completely. Do these change the meaning in any way?

Independent work

- Children answer the questions about the extract.

Plenary

- Review the children's independent text work.

DAY 2

Big Book 4B pp.44-46; Pupil's Book p.63

Shared reading

- Look at the use of paragraphs. Ask the children to identify the main idea of each one.
- Ask the children to read the passage aloud, with intonation and expression appropriate to the grammar and punctuation.
- Which words anticipate that something is about to happen? What do the children think will happen next?
- Introduce the children to the cloze passage from *The Hobbit,* on page 63 in the pupil's book. Remind the children of the importance of reading the words before and after the missing word, when looking for clues.

Focused word/sentence work

- Notice the use of the apostrophe for possession in 'the valley's edge'.
- Ask the children to define words from the passage in as few words as they can, e.g. railway, patch, pit, narrow, peered, wrong, etc.

Independent work

- Children work on the cloze passage from *The Hobbit* on page 63 in the pupil's book.

Plenary

- Review the children's suggestions for the cloze passage. Any word which fits the sense is acceptable, but the words used by the author are given here for reference purposes: dirty, an, hole, on, round, knob, door, very, floors, lots, tunnel, side, people, first, bedrooms, clothes, same.

DAY 3

Big Book 4B pp.44-46; Pupil's Book p.64

Shared reading and writing, including focused word/sentence work

- Compare the setting in this extract with those in earlier units. How are they similar/different? Which do the children prefer? Why?
- Read the extract again. Focus on how the setting is built up using detail. Make a list of words and phrases which the author uses. Which of these create moods and arouse expectations?
- Discuss the use of adjectival phrases and similes in the text, e.g. with precipices on either side, like a huge pit or trench.
- Look at the scene showing an imaginary land on page 64 in the pupil's book. Encourage the children to brainstorm suitable words and phrases to describe what they see there, perhaps using similar descriptive language to that of the extract in the anthology.
- Experiment with words which will create moods and arouse expectations.
- Work together to write a description of the scene.

Independent work

- Children begin work on their own descriptive writing.

Plenary

- Review the work in progress, offering help and encouragement.

DAY 4

Big Book 4B pp.47-48; Pupil's Book p.64

Shared reading

- Read the second extract from *The Voyage of the Dawn Treader*. Is this what the children expected would happen? Look back at the earlier extract. What clues are there which suggest there might be a dragon in the cave? e.g. the black burnt patches on the ground, the two thin wisps of smoke coming from the cave.
- Focus on the description of the dragon. Ask the children to identify the adjectives, the adjectival phrases, and the simile. Which lines confirm that the two wisps of smoke seen earlier were indeed coming from the dragon?
- What was unusual about this dragon? How did Eustace feel as he watched it move?

Focused word/sentence work

- Ask the children to define words from the passage in as few words as possible, e.g. cave, elbow, wings, smoke, surprised, behaviour, pool, pause, etc.

Independent work

- Children complete their descriptive writing and/or begin a story using the setting they have described.

Plenary

- Ask the children to read aloud some of their descriptions.

DAY 5

Big Book 4B pp.44-48; Pupil's Book p.64

Shared reading

- What is the main idea of each paragraph? Which details support each main idea?
- How does the text make the children feel? Ask them to explain why they feel that way.
- What do they think will happen next? Ask them to justify their answers, using detail from the text to support their ideas.

Focused word/sentence work

- Ask the children to identify uses of the apostrophe to denote possession.
- Revise the use of the apostrophe to denote missing letters in contractions. Ensure the children are able to distinguish between the two uses.
- Discuss the differences between *its* and *it's*. Which shows possession and which denotes a contraction? Why might this be confusing? Ask the children to identify examples of *its* in the text.

Independent work

- Children consolidate their understanding of the use of the apostrophe to denote possession, and to revise its use in contractions.

Plenary

- Review the week's work, re-emphasising teaching points and clarifying misconceptions.

Consolidation and extension

- Ask the children to prepare and read aloud their descriptions.
- Record the children's descriptions and stories on tape.
- Collect other examples of descriptions of settings in fantasy adventures.

Homework

- Page 21 in the homework book focuses on proofreading for spelling and punctuation errors.

ASSESSMENT

Copymaster 20 is an assessment master of key word and sentence objectives for term 2, testing the children's ability to define words, to re-order sentences to retain and change meaning, and to construct adjectival phrases and interesting sentences. Indirectly, it will also test vocabulary, spelling and handwriting. The completed sheet will be useful as a record of progress, together with examples of the pupil's text work.

HALF-TERMLY PLANNER

Year 4 • Term 3 • Weeks 1–5

SCHOOL ____________________ **CLASS** ________ **TEACHER** ____________

		Phonetics, spelling and vocabulary	Grammar and punctuation	Comprehension and composition	Texts
Continuous work					**Range**
Weeks 1–5		WL 1, 2, 3, 4, 13, 14			**Fiction and Poetry:** stories/short novels that raise issues; stories by same author; stories from other cultures. Range of poetry in different forms **Non-fiction:** information books linked to other curricular areas
Blocked work					
Week	**Unit**				**Titles**
1	**21**	WL 5, 6	SL 3, 4	TL 1, 2, 3, 8, 10, 11	extracts from *Kamla and Kate*, Jamila Gavin
2	**22**	WL 5, 10	SL 1, 3	TL 1, 3, 8, 9	extracts from *Goggle-Eyes*, Anne Fine
3	**23**	WL 8, 9	SL 1	TL 1, 4, 8, 9, 11, 12	extract from *Gowie Corby Plays Chicken*, Gene Kemp and the poem 'I've Got an Apple Ready', John Herbert Walsh
4	**24**	WL 6, 12	SL 2	TL 4, 5, 6, 7, 9, 14, 15	poems: 'All for an ice-cream', Karen Jackson; 'I'm the youngest in our house', Michael Rosen; from 'Skipping Song', John Herbert Walsh; 'Jetsam', Nigel Cox
5	**25**	WL 6, 9	SL 4	TL 16, 17, 18, 20, 21, 23, 24	extract from *Waste and Recycling*, Barbara Taylor, and the poem 'The Tree House', Stanley Cook

Focus on Literacy Teacher's Resource Book 4 © Barry and Anita Scholes, HarperCollins*Publishers* Ltd 1999

HALF-TERMLY PLANNER

Year 4 • Term 3 • Weeks 6–10

SCHOOL ____________________ **CLASS** ________ **TEACHER** ____________

		Phonetics, spelling and vocabulary	Grammar and punctuation	Comprehension and composition	Texts
Continuous work **Weeks 6–10**		WL 1, 2, 3, 4, 13, 14			**Range** **Fiction and poetry:** stories/short novels that raise issues; stories from other cultures. Range of poetry in different forms **Non-fiction:** persuasive writing: adverts, circulars, flyers; discussion texts: debates, editorials
Blocked work					
Week	**Unit**				**Titles**
6	**26**	WL 7	SL 3, 4	TL 16, 17, 18, 20, 21, 22, 23, 24	flyer: 'Cruelty to Circus Animals'; letter to a newspaper editor; discussion text: 'Pets'
7	**27**	WL 8	SL 1, 3, 4	TL 1, 2, 3, 8	extracts from *Journey to Jo'burg*, Beverley Naidoo
8	**28**	WL 11	SL 2	TL 1, 3, 8, 13	extracts from *The Meteorite Spoon*, Philip Ridley
9	**29**	—	SL 3	TL 18, 19, 25	Advertisements: Crunchy Wheat; Robo; slogans and jingles
10	**30**	WL 7	SL 1	TL 4, 5, 6, 7, 14, 15	poems: 'Black Dot', Libby Houston; 'Quao', Pamela Mordecai; 'Fish', John Cunliffe; 'Winter Morning', Ogden Nash; 'Storm', Wes Magee; two epitaphs, Anon; 'Happy Haiku', James Kirkup

Unit 21 The New Boy

Key Learning Objectives

TL1	To identify social, moral or cultural issues in stories, e.g. the dilemmas faced by characters or the moral of the story, and to discuss how the characters deal with them, to locate evidence in the text
TL2	To read stories from other cultures, by focusing on, e.g. differences in place, time, customs, relationships; to identify and discuss recurring themes where appropriate
TL3	To understand how paragraphs or chapters are used to collect, order and build up ideas
TL8	To write critically about an issue or dilemma raised in the story, explaining the problem and alternative courses of action
TL10	To describe and review own reading habits and to widen experience
TL11	To explore the main issues of a story by writing a story about a dilemma and the issues it raises for the character
SL3	To understand how the grammar of a sentence alters when a positive statement is made negative
SL4	To use connectives, e.g. adverbs, adverbial phrases, conjunctions, to structure an argument: if . . . then
WL5	To explore the occurrence of certain letters: 'v' and 'k' and the letter strings 'wa', and 'wo' within words; deduce some of the conventions for using them at the beginnings of words
WL6	To spell words with common letter strings but different pronunciations

Range:	Story that raises an issue
Texts:	Extracts from *Kamla and Kate*, Jamila Gavin
Resources:	Big Book 4C pp.4-8 Pupil's Book 4 pp.65-67 Homework Book 4 p.22: Missing letters – *v, k, wo* and *wa* Copymaster 21: Reading record

DAY 1

Big Book 4C pp.4-6; Pupil's Book pp.65-66

Shared reading

- What issue does this story raise? It may be that there is someone in the class, or the school, who has faced similar problems. Most children will remember feeling lost and confused when beginning school, or changing to a different school. How much more difficult is it then for Amrik? Ask the children to consider the special problems facing him: everything is different, puzzling and rather frightening, and only Kamla can speak his language.
- A few children in the class may have looked after new entrants to the school, but consider the extra responsibility placed on Kamla as the only person who can communicate with Amrik, guide him, calm his fears and help him make new friends. Discuss the help she has given him already and what else she might do.
- How does Amrik feel? Ask the children to look for evidence in the text.

Focused word/sentence work

- Compare the word 'wear' with 'hear'. The two words have a similar spelling pattern, but different pronunciations. Pick out other words from the text which show this, e.g. stood (mood); there (here); said (paid); wall (shall); live (alive, live); grow (how); stone (one).
- Consider the word 'earth' which has the same sound as 'birth', but a different spelling. Pick out other words from the text which show this, e.g. socks (box); sky (lie, bye, buy, high); there (hair, tear); grey (say, eat, meet).

Independent work

- Children answer the questions about the text.

Plenary

- Review the children's independent text work. Revise how to use the text to find literal answers, and how to use clues where information is not given directly.

DAY 2

Big Book 4C pp.4-6; Pupil's Book p.66

Shared reading

- Find the clues in the text which reveal the differences between Amrik's life in India and his new life. Discuss the contrasts. Ask the class to find out about mangoes and guavas.
- Examine the use of paragraphs in the text. Which paragraph best reveals Amrik's thoughts and feelings? Look at the words which link the classroom events to those in the playground: 'At playtime . . .'. Consider the final three paragraphs and point out that a new paragraph is begun for each speaker.

Focused word/sentence work

- Ask the children to find the word 'plough' in the text. Collect other 'ough' words, e.g. tough, through, though, cough. Point out that although they have the same phoneme, the words are pronounced differently.
- Explore compound words: everyone, playtime, playground, wheatfields, countryside; and shorter words within the letters of longer ones: village, table, prodded, wear, etc.

Independent work

- Page 66 in the pupil's book has a continuation of the story presented as a cloze passage. All the missing words are verbs, giving opportunity for the children to understand the need for grammatical agreement.

Plenary

- Review the children's cloze work. For reference purposes the actual words used by the author are: dragged, taking, drink, watched, pressed, arched, seen, asked, said, comes, pulled, murmured, be, passed, was, enjoyed, say, is, are, am, learnt.

DAY 3

Big Book 4C pp.4-6; Pupil's Book p.67

Shared reading and writing, including focused word/sentence work

- Identify the differences in culture between India and England, using evidence from the text. Discuss how this made Amrik's first day so bewildering.
- Ask the children to imagine they have moved to a new school in a different country. What problems might they face because of different customs, language, facilities. How would they deal with them?
- Plan together the story of that first day, using the ideas on page 67 of the pupil's book.
- Make a list of words from the text which you might use in your own writing to show how you feel and behave, e.g. awkwardly, frightened, puzzled, despair.
- Make a list of questions you might ask of your interpreter.

Independent work

- Children begin their own story.

Plenary

- Review the work in progress, offering help and encouragement.

DAY 4

Big Book 4C pp.7-8; Pupil's Book p.67

Shared reading

- Kamla is unable to interpret for Amrik at lunch time, so she asks her English friend Kate to look after him. How might this make it more difficult for Amrik?
- Encourage the children to put themselves in his place and to explain the problem Amrik faced in the dining-room and why he behaved the way he did. Why did he not use his knife and fork?
- What do the children think of Kate's attempt to look after the new boy? How might she have looked after him better?

Focused word/sentence work

- Use the connectives 'if' or 'then' to explore alternative outcomes, e.g. if Kamla had been able to sit with Amrik then . . .; if Amrik had already known how to use a knife and fork then . . . ; if Kate had paid more attention to Amrik then . . .
- Ask the children to identify words which use the apostrophe. In each case, is it used to denote possession or contraction?

Independent work

- Children continue their story writing

Plenary

- Review the children's writing, reading aloud examples in order to draw attention to good practice.

DAY 5

Big Book 4C pp.4-8; Pupil's Book p.67

Shared reading

- Ask the children to identify from the description in the text what the food on Amrik's plate might have been.
- Explore the use of paragraphs in the text. What is the main idea of each one? Why are there four paragraphs which consist of a single sentence? Remind the children that when writing dialogue they should begin a new paragraph for each new speaker.

Focused word/sentence work

- Explore the occurrence of the letter string *wa* in *watched,* and in *water* and *walked* in the earlier extract. Ask the children to suggest other words which contain this letter string, e.g. watch, swat, warm.
- Page 22 in the homework book explores *wa, wo, k* and *v*.
- Investigate positive and negative sentences. Ask the children to identify the negative sentences in the text. Experiment with ways of changing positive to negative and vice versa. Notice the change in words required when changing 'He hadn't eaten a thing' into a positive sentence.

Independent work

- Children explore positive and negative sentences.

Plenary

- Review the week's work, consolidating teaching points.

Consolidation and extension

- Children prepare and read aloud their stories.
- Hold a discussion on the issues explored in the children's writing.
- Copymaster 21 is a reading record sheet for the children to note the titles of books, comics, magazines, newspapers, etc., that they read. Encourage the children to discuss their reading habits, and to use the sheet to see how and where they might widen their reading experience.

Homework

- Page 22 in the homework book focuses on the occurrence of the letters *k* and *v* and the letter strings *wa* and *wo*.

Unit 22

Mum's New Boyfriend

Key Learning Objectives

TL1 To identify social, moral or cultural issues in stories, e.g. the dilemmas faced by characters or the moral of the story, and to discuss how the characters deal with them, to locate evidence in the text

TL3 To understand how paragraphs or chapters are used to collect, order and build up ideas

TL8 To write critically about an issue or dilemma raised in the story, explaining the problem, alternative courses of action and evaluating the writer's solution

TL9 To read further stories or poems by a favourite writer, making comparisons and identifying familiar features of the writer's work

SL1 To understand that some words can be changed in particular ways and others cannot: changing verb endings, adding comparative endings, pluralisation and that these are important clues for identifying word classes

SL3 To understand how the grammar of a sentence alters when the sentence type is altered: a statement is made into a question, a question becomes an order noting:

- the order of words
- additions and/or deletions of words
- changes to punctuation

WL5 To explore the occurrence of *'ss'* within words; deduce some of the conventions for using them at the middles and endings of words

WL10 To distinguish the two forms: *its* (possessive no apostrophe) and *it's* (contracted *it is*) and to use these accurately in own writing

Range:	Short novel that raises an issue; stories by the same author
Texts:	Extracts from *Goggle-Eyes*, Anne Fine
Resources:	Big Book 4C pp.9-13 Pupil's Book 4 pp.68-70 Homework Book 4 p.23: words with 'ss' Copymaster 22: Comparing books by the same author

Preparation

- Make available other books by Anne Fine for comparison, or refer to the extract from *A Sudden Glow of Gold* (Collins Focus on Literacy 3, Unit 28).

DAY 1

Big Book 4C pp.9-11; Pupil's Book pp.68-69

Shared reading

- What is the issue raised in this story? Ask the children to describe Kitty's behaviour. Why is she behaving that way? Compare her behaviour with that of her sister. Why is Judith behaving differently? Have any children in the class been in a similar situation? How did they feel and behave?
- Read the text a second time, examining how Kitty reveals her attitude to Gerald. What does her first impression tell us? Who might Simon be? What is the only thing about Gerald which Kitty finds in his favour? (The box of chocolates.) How did she avoid shaking hands? Why did she do this? Why did she decide not to talk to him? What must Gerald have thought of Kitty's behaviour? What might the consequences of such behaviour be?

Focused word/sentence work

- Investigate synonymous verbs, by experimenting with subsituting other verbs for those in the passage, e.g. stepped, shifted, sidled, smiled, rushed, clutching, swivelled, inspect, etc. What effect on meaning do the substitutions have?

Independent work

- Children answer the questions on the text.

Plenary

- Review the children's independent text work.

DAY 2

Big Book 4C pp.9-11; Pupil's Book p.69

Shared reading

- Discuss the greetings used when Gerald met the children. How might they have greeted each other differently?
- Kitty's prejudice against Gerald makes her question his motive for everything he says and does. What do the children think of her reasoning? Might there be some truth in it? Can the class suggest any other explanations?
- What would the children have done if they were Kitty?
- Compare this story by Anne Fine with the extract from her book *A Sudden Glow of Gold* (Collins Focus on Literacy 3, Unit 28).
- Copymaster 22 is a book review for comparing two books by the same author. Ask the children to use cover information and other sources to find out about the author.

Focused word/sentence work

- Experiment with sentence transformations: statements into questions and vice versa, positives into negatives and vice versa. Ask the children to turn Gerald's 'It looks as if it might be you' into a question, a negative and a certainty.
- Explore how questions can be changed into orders, and what words need to be added or deleted.

Independent work

- Children explore sentence transformations: changing statements into questions, and vice versa, and questions into orders, and vice versa.

Plenary

- Review the children's sentence transformations, re-emphasising teaching points and clarifying misconceptions.

DAY 3

Big Book 4C pp.9-13; Pupil's Book p.70

Shared reading and writing, including focused word/sentence work

- Read the first extract again and then the second extract, which continues the story.
- Discuss Kitty's attitude to Gerald. What clues does she pick up about him from what he says and does? Is she being fair?
- Tell the children that they are going to write about Kitty and her problem with Mum's new boyfriend.
- Plan the writing in four paragraphs as outlined on page 70 of the pupil's book. Make notes of the children's ideas, explaining the problem and evaluating Kitty's approach to it.
- Consider the possible advantages and disadvantages of the situation. Encourage the children to use connectives to structure this, e.g. if, then, on the other hand.
- Discuss alternative actions that Kitty might take.

Independent work

- Children begin their writing about Kitty.

Plenary

- Review the work in progress, offering help and encouragement.

DAY 4

Big Book 4C pp.9-13; Pupil's Book p.70

Shared reading

- What does the class think Gerald meant by 'Who's a *nice* Kitty?' What different interpretations might it have? Kitty isn't sure what he meant. From what the children know about Kitty, what interpretation is she likely to put on it when she has time to work it out?
- Kitty and her sister are meeting Gerald for the first time, but at the end of the extract Kitty realises that Gerald has been in their house before. What clues are there to this? How might it change her attitude to him? Why do they think Mum had not told them about an earlier visit?

Focused word/sentence work

- Ask the children to identify five common nouns, five adjectives and five verbs from the passage.
- Experiment with changing these words. Can the nouns be made plural? Or plural nouns be made singular? How can this be done? Can the tense of the verbs be changed? In what way? Might comparative endings be added to the adjectives?
- Explain that these are all important clues for identifying word classes.

Independent work

- Children complete their writing, or use their ideas to continue the story of Kitty and Gerald.

Plenary

- Discuss the children's evaluations of Kitty and her problem.

DAY 5

Big Book 4C pp.9-13; Pupil's Book p.70

Shared reading

- Ask the children to retell the events of the story from the different points of view of Kitty, her sister Jude, and Gerald.
- Gerald's point of view is perhaps the most interesting. What might he really think about Kitty? How much might he already know about her? Might he have been warned by Mum to expect such behaviour? How does he feel about it? Might Kitty be right in thinking he is cunning?

Focused word/sentence work

- Ask the children to identify the occurrence of *its* and *it's* in the passage. Distinguish between the two, and let the children know that this is a particularly common confusion.

Independent work

- Children distinguish between *its* and *it's*.

Plenary

- Review the week's work, re-emphasising teaching points and clarifying misconceptions.

Consolidation and extension

- Copymaster 22 is a book review for comparing two books by the same author. Ask the children to use cover information and other sources to find out about the author.
- Discuss the similarities and differences between books by the same author.

Homework

- Page 23 in the homework book focuses on the letter string *ss*.

Unit 23

The Attack

Key Learning Objectives

TL1	To identify social, moral or cultural issues in stories, e.g. the dilemmas faced by characters or the moral of the story, and to discuss how the characters deal with them, to locate evidence in the text
TL4	To understand the following terms and identify them in poems: 'verse', 'stanza', 'rhyme', 'rhythm'
TL8	To write critically about an issue or dilemma raised in the story, explaining the problem, alternative courses of action and evaluating the writer's solution
TL9	To read further poems by a favourite writer, making comparisons and identifying familiar features of the writer's work
TL11	To explore the main issues of a story by writing a story about a dilemma and the issues it raises for the character
TL12	To write an alternative ending for a known story and discuss how this would change the reader's view of the characters and events of the original story
SL1	To understand that some words can be changed in particular ways and others cannot, e.g. changing verb endings, adding comparative endings, pluralisation and that these are important clues for identifying word classes
WL8	To practise extending and compounding words through adding parts; revise and reinforce earlier work (Y3) on suffixes; investigate links between meaning and spelling
WL9	To recognise and spell the suffixes *-ible, -able, -ive, -tion, -sion*

Range:	Story that raises an issue Monologue poem which also raises an issue
Texts:	Extract from *Gowie Corby Plays Chicken*, Gene Kemp 'I've Got an Apple Ready', John Herbert Walsh
Resources:	Big Book 4C pp.14-17 Pupil's Book 4 pp.71-73 Homework Book 4 p.24: Suffixes *-ful, -fully, ive, -tion, -ly, -less, -or, -er, -est,* and *-ness.* Copymaster 23: Book review: a story that raises an issue Copymaster 24: Book review: plot

DAY 1

Big Book 4C pp.14-15; Pupil's Book pp.71-72

Shared reading

- What is the issue in this story? Why is Gowie being attacked? Can the attack be justified? What alternative course of action might the attackers have taken? Ask the children to give reasons for their answers.
- How does Gowie feel before the attack? Why does he feel like this? This feeling is changed mid-sentence. Which words show the change? This particular sentence begins with Gowie opening the door, on the very point of reaching safety, and ends with the attack. The unexpectedness of the attack is made stronger by the author's mid-sentence surprise for the reader. The words then spill on, uninterrupted, like the series of blows they describe.
- Why does the writer choose to put Gowie's return home and the attack on him in the same paragraph? Experiment with separating these events. Where would the new paragraph begin? Is this change more, or less, effective? Why?

Focused word/sentence work

- Why does the class think the author has chosen to write in the present tense? Experiment with changing it into the past tense. Compare the two versions. Which works best? Why?
- Investigate the words used in the description of the attack, e.g. crash, stab, bam, bang, all hell breaks loose, pain swells, jumped, ambushed, hitting, kicking, tears, gashes, scrunch, scrape, etc.
- Consider the verb endings: -ed, -ing, -s, -es. Experiment with changing verbs by adding endings, e.g. jump, jumps, jumped, jumping; ambush, ambushes, ambushed, ambushing. Test other verbs to see if they can be changed in this way.

Independent work

- Children answer the questions on the text.

Plenary

- Review the children's independent text work.

DAY 2

Big Book 4C pp.14-15; Pupil's Book p.72

Shared reading

- Look at the sentence beginning 'Blood and salt in my mouth . . .' What does it tell us about Gowie's feelings and thoughts? Why does the class think the author makes this one long sentence instead of several short ones? What is the effect of the suspension points, e.g. 'lie still . . . play dead . . . lie still . . . lie dead . . .'?
- How does Gowie respond to the attack? What do his attackers say which shows how they feel? Would they have continued if someone had not called out to them? What might the consequences of the attack be?
- Is it likely Gowie's attitude to the other children might be changed by the attack? Ask the children to explain how this might be.
- Ask the children whom Gowie is supposed to have hurt. How can they tell? Who among the attackers says they have gone too far? Discuss reasons why this should be one and the same person.

Focused word/sentence work

- Investigate the use of suffixes in words in the text, e.g. stretch<u>ing</u>, sudden<u>ly</u>, jump<u>ed</u>, anx<u>ious</u>,

- Introduce the children to other suffixes: *-ful, -ly, -ic, -ist, -ible, -able, -ive, -tion, -sion.*
- Ask the children to find words ending in these, or to make words from root words, e.g. prevention, panic, hopeful. Discuss words which drop letters before adding a suffix, e.g. confusion, operation, pianist.
- Investigate which endings make adjectives, nouns and adverbs.

Independent work

- Children practise extending and compounding words through adding suffixes: *-ful, -ly, -ic, -ist, -ible, -able, -ive, -tion, -sion.*

Plenary

- Discuss the children's work on suffixes. Which endings make adjectives, nouns, adverbs? Investigate links between meaning and spelling.

DAY 3

Big Book 4C pp.14-15; Pupil's Book p.73

Shared reading and writing

- Ask the children to retell the story from the different points of view of Gowie, the attackers, and Rosie Lee.
- Discuss alternative possible endings to the story. Consider the questions on page 73 in the pupil's book. Make notes of the children's responses.
- Discuss which alternative ending would be the most satisfactory, and why.
- Plan the ending in four paragraphs: introduction, build-up, climax and resolution.

Focused word/sentence work

- Discuss the use of the first person and present tense in the children's writing.

Independent work

- Children begin work on their ending to the story.

Plenary

- Review the work in progress, offering help and encouragement.

DAY 4

Big Book 4C pp.16-17; Pupil's Book p.73

Shared reading

- Read the monologue poem 'I've Got an Apple Ready'. What is the issue here? How do we know the victim in the poem is a girl? How does she feel about being bullied? Which words give clues?
- What is her solution to the problem? How effective is it? What else might she do? What might the consequences of such an action be?
- What would the children do in a similar situation?
- Introduce the children to the terms 'monologue' and 'stanza'.
- Investigate the pattern of the poem. How many stanzas does it have? What is its rhyming pattern?

Focused word/sentence work

- The poem is written mainly in the present tense. In which stanzas is the future tense used?
- What are 'pit-a-pat feet'. Discuss the use of onomatopeoia.

Independent work

- Children continue their writing. Those who finish might write a short newspaper-style report about the incident, following the suggestions in the pupil's book.

Plenary

- Review the children's writing. Discuss the issues it raises.

DAY 5

Big Book 4C pp.14-17; Pupil's Book p.73

Shared reading

- Ask what the poem tells us about Bill Craddock. Why might his eyes be 'somehow sad'?
- Discuss reasons why Bill Craddock might behave in the way he does.
- Is his bullying as bad as the attack on Gowie? Ask the children to justify their answers.
- Which behaviour is more likely to continue: that of Bill Craddock or Gowie's attackers? What makes the children think so?

Focused word/sentence work

- Experiment with changing verb endings, e.g. want, wanted, wanting; get, got, getting.
- Ask the children to identify the nouns and to use the pluralisation test on each one, e.g. bow, bows; satchel, satchels; tooth, teeth. Ask which nouns are already plural, e.g. feet, workmen.
- Ask the children to identify adjectives in the text. Experiment with adding comparative endings, e.g. slow, slower, slowest.
- Remind the children that the above are important clues for identifying word classes.

Independent work

- Children write a letter to the girl in the poem, saying what she should do about Bill Craddock and why.

Plenary

- Review the week's work, consolidating teaching points.

Consolidation and extension

- Let the children prepare and read aloud their letters and their own endings to the story about Gowie.
- Find a copy of 'The Bully Asleep' by John Herbert Walsh. The poem is in *Poets in Hand*, Puffin. It tells what happens when the children in his class find Bill Craddock asleep. Compare the two poems, identifying familiar features.
- Copymaster 23 is a book review which focuses on stories that raise issues.
- Copymaster 24 is a book review focusing on the build-up and climax of a story.

Homework

- Page 24 in the homework book gives practice in extending words using the suffixes *-ful, -fully, -ive, -tion, -ly, -less, -or, -er, -est,* and *-ness.*

Unit 24

Conversation Poems

Key Learning Objectives

TL4	To understand the following terms and identify them in poems: 'verse', 'rhyme', 'rhythm'
TL5	To clap out and count the syllables in each line of regular poetry
TL6	To describe how a poet does or does not use rhyme
TL7	To recognise some simple forms of poetry and their uses: the regularity of skipping songs
TL9	To read further stories or poems by a favourite writer, making comparisons and identifying familiar features of the writer's work
TL14	To write poems, experimenting with different styles and structures, discuss if and why different forms are more suitable than others
TL15	To produce polished poetry through revision, e.g. deleting words, adding words, changing words, reorganising words and lines, experimenting with figurative language
SL2	To identify the common punctuation marks including commas, semi-colons, colons, dashes, hyphens, speech marks, and to respond to them appropriately when reading
WL6	To spell words with common letter strings but different pronunciations
WL12	To understand how diminutives are formed

Range:	Conversation poems; list poem; skipping song
Texts:	'All for an ice-cream', Karen Jackson; 'I'm the youngest in our house', Michael Rosen; 'Jetsam', Nigel Cox; from 'Skipping Song', John Herbert Walsh
Resources:	Big Book 4C pp.18-21 Pupil's Book 4 pp.74-76 Homework Book 4 p.25: Spelling and sound

DAY 1

Big Book 4C pp.18-19; Pupil's Book pp.74-75

Shared reading

- Read the poems aloud. Do the poems sound made up or could the conversation have actually happened?
- Do the poems remind the children of any conversations they have had with adults and other children. Encourage the children to note these down for the writing on days 3 and 4.
- What do the children find amusing about the poems? Which part is the most humorous? Why?
- Why is the last line of Michael Rosen's poem written in capital letters?
- How does the boy in that poem feel? How might the child in Karen Jackson's poem feel? Might she feel differently as time passes? Why?
- How can we tell that Karen Jackson's poem was written some time ago? (A 10p ice-cream). How much would it be today?

Focused word/sentence work

- Explore the use of speech marks. The Michael Rosen poem introduces each speech to make it clear who is speaking. 'All for an ice-cream' consists only of the spoken words. How can we tell who is speaking?
- Investigate the use of punctuation: speech marks, commas, question and exclamation marks, the colon, hyphens, dashes. Explain the functions of the ones the children are unclear about. Demonstrate this by reading appropriate parts out loud.

Independent work

- Children answer questions on the poems.

Plenary

- Review the children's independent text work.

DAY 2

Big Book 4C pp.18-19; Pupil's Book p.75

Shared reading

- Ask the children to read the poems out loud with one child for each speaker. Encourage them to use the punctuation to help them perform the poem appropriately.
- Look at the pattern of the poems. How are they set out? Do they rhyme? Why is the fact that they do not rhyme not really important? What is important in a conversation poem? (That the conversation sounds natural and interesting).
- Which poem do the children like best? Why?

Focused word/sentence work

- Ask the children to suggest words which rhyme with *fluff*. Encourage them to continue until they suggest one with the *ough* letter string, e.g. enough, tough, rough.
- Investigate the spelling of words with this common letter string but different pronunciations, e.g. tough, trough, dough, plough, through, thorough.
- Make a list of these words and ask the children to use them in sentences.

Independent work

- Children investigate the spelling of words with the *ough* letter string.

Plenary

- Review the children's independent work, re-emphasising teaching points and clarifying misconceptions.

DAY 3

Big Book 4C pp.20-21; Pupil's Book p.76

Shared reading and writing, including focused word/sentence work

- Read the poems 'Jetsam' and 'Skipping Song'.
- Investigate the pattern of the poems. How are they similar? How are they different? Do they rhyme? Notice the internal rhymes of 'Jetsam'. Do they have strong rhythms? Ask the children to clap out the rhythm and count the syllables.
- What is jetsam? 'Jetsam' is a list poem, each item chosen to fit the rhythm.
- Use one of the poems on this page, or one of the conversation poems on the previous pages, as a model for a shared poem.
- Use the ideas in the pupil's book to start you off. Brainstorm further ideas.

Independent work

- Children begin writing their own poems.

Plenary

- Review the work in progress. Discuss how the poems might be improved by deleting, adding or changing words. Explore the effects of changing the order of words or lines. Examine the use of similes. Where might they be used to best effect?

DAY 4

Big Book 4C pp.18-21; Pupil's Book p.76

Shared reading and writing

- Experiment with improvements to the shared poem you wrote together on day 4. Try deleting, adding or changing words. Explore the effects of changing the order of words or lines. Experiment with figurative language.
- Why does a skipping rhyme need a strong rhythm? Would 'Jetsam' make a suitable skipping rhyme? Ask the children to justify their answers.

Focused word/sentence work

- Investigate the use of punctuation: commas, colons, semi-colons and hyphens in the poems.
- Ask the children to read the poems out loud, responding to the punctuation appropriately.

Independent work

- Encourage the children to revise and improve their poems. Those who finish might begin a second poem in a different form.

Plenary

- Discuss the children's poems. How might they be improved? Is the form suitable for its purpose? Ask the children to justify their answers.

DAY 5

Big Book 4C pp.18-21; Pupil's Book p.76

Shared reading

- 'Skipping Song' is another poem by John Herbert Walsh (see 'I've Got an Apple Ready' in Unit 23). Compare the two poems. Discuss the differences. Which do the children prefer? Why?
- Which of the poems in this unit do the children prefer? Why? Ask them to read aloud their favourites.

Focused word/sentence work

- Ask the children to identify the synonyms for *small* in 'Skipping Song'. What other synonyms can they suggest?
- Discuss how diminutives are formed by the use of suffixes, e.g. *-ette* (launderette, cassette); *-et* (droplet, leaflet); *-ling* (sapling, changeling). The prefix *mini-* is often used too, e.g. minibus, mini-market.
- Discuss the use of adding *'y'* to personal names to make a diminutive, e.g. Jonesy.
- Ask the children to identify the shortened or pet names for common personal names, e.g. Dan or Danny from Daniel.

Independent work

- Children explore how diminutives are formed.

Plenary

- Review the week's work, consolidating teaching points.

Consolidation and extension

- Encourage the children to perform their own poems and the poems in this unit.
- Ask the children to collect skipping rhymes for their own anthology.
- Encourage the children to read more poems by Michael Rosen about everyday family situations. What are the familiar features of the writer's work?

Homework

- Page 25 in the homework book encourages the children to explore more words with the same spelling pattern, but different pronunciations.

Unit 25 Paper

Key Learning Objectives

TL16 To read, compare and evaluate examples of arguments and discussions

TL17 To investigate how arguments are presented, e.g. ordering points to link them together so that one follows from another; how statistics can be used to support arguments

TL18 From examples of persuasive writing, to investigate how style and vocabulary are used to convince the intended reader

TL20 To summarise a sentence or paragraph by identifying the most important elements and rewording them in a limited number of words

TL21 To assemble and sequence points in order to plan the presentation of a point of view

TL23 To present a point of view in writing, linking points persuasively and selecting style and vocabulary appropriate to the reader

TL24 To summarise in writing the key ideas

SL4 To use connectives, e.g. adverbs, adverbial phrases, conjunctions, to structure an argument

WL6 To spell words with common letter strings but different pronunciations

WL9 To recognise and spell the suffixes *-ible, -able, -ive, -tion, -sion*

Range:	Persuasive writing from an information book; poem
Texts:	Extract from *Waste and Recycling*, Barbara Taylor 'The Tree House', Stanley Cook
Resources:	Big Book 4C pp.22-25 Pupil's Book 4 pp.77-79 Homework Book 4 p.26: Word endings: *-ble, -able, -tion, -sion, -ive, -our, -ough, -ould*

Preparation

NB: In this unit, writing activities take place on days 2, 3 and 4.

- You may wish to compare 'The Tree House' by Stanley Cook with the poem 'In the Wood' by Sheila Simmons, from Unit 13 (see day 5.)

DAY 1

Big Book 4C pp.22-23; Pupil's Book pp.77-78

Shared reading

- What is the issue the text presents? Examine how it is presented:

  an introduction which clearly states the issue;
  numbered points describing the paper-making process and its energy, water and chemical requirements;
  a conclusion which suggests an alternative course of action to alleviate the problem.
- Explain how the numbered points link the arguments together so that one follows from another.
- Ask the children to identify the statistics which support the argument, e.g. every year, each one of us uses up to two trees' worth of paper and cardboard.
- Ask the children to explain in their own words how the paper-making process impacts on the environment.

Focused word/sentence work

- Investigate the apostrophe in 'two trees' worth'. What is its function: to show possession or contraction? Why does the apostrophe come after the s?
- Examine the final sentence, which begins, 'If paper is recycled . . .' Even though the word 'then' is missing, this is an 'If . . . then' construction. Test this by adding 'then' after the comma.
- Ask the children to identify a word with the suffix *-tion* (pollution). What kind of word is this? From what verb does it come?

Independent work

- Children answer questions on the text.

Plenary

- Review the children's independent text work.

DAY 2

Big Book 4C pp.22-23; Pupil's Book p.78

Shared reading and writing

- The independent work for day 2 is a writing activity on the advantages of recycling paper. Read the text again for information which will help the children to do this.
- Ask the children to explain the advantages of paper re-cycling. Make notes.
- Discuss ways in which the children can help to save and recycle paper. Make notes of their ideas.

Focused word/sentence work

- Experiment with changing the word order in sentences in the text. Which sentences need additions or deletions?
- Experiment with changing statements into questions. Discuss the changes required to do this, e.g. word order, additions/deletions of words, changes to punctuation.

Independent work

- Children write about the advantages of recycling paper. This may need further time outside the literacy hour.

Plenary

- Review the children's writing. Are their ideas presented clearly, with points ordered and properly linked together? Have they used facts and figures to support their argument? Does the conclusion sum up their argument?

DAY 3

Big Book 4C pp.22-23; Pupil's Book p.79

Shared reading and writing including focused word/sentence work

- Investigate how style and vocabulary are used to convince the intended reader. The text consists of factual sentences, without any of the opinions of the writer. Each sentence uses the minimum words to make its point. Ask the children to check this by summarising some of the sentences. Statistics are used to support the argument. The points follow one from another, building to a logical conclusion, again supported by facts and figures. Technical words are used, e.g. pollution, energy, recycled. Does the writer expect the reader to be familiar with such words? Are these words necessary? Do they make the argument more, or less, convincing? Why?
- Look at page 79 in the pupil's book. Ask the children to choose an issue they feel strongly about. Discuss their points of view. Make notes. If necessary make two lists, one for and one against. Distinguish between fact and opinion. Make sure the children understand that facts are more persuasive than opinions.
- Use the plan in the pupil's book to structure the ideas. If you have an issue on which the children's opinions are divided, then focus on just one side of the argument. Decide on the audience for the children's writing. Who are they trying to convince, other children or adults? How will this affect the style and vocabulary of their writing?
- Discuss ways of introducing the reader to the issue, perhaps by using statistics.
- Discuss ways of ordering the children's ideas so that they follow logically from one point to the next, e.g. numbered points, using connecting words and phrases (see the list in the pupil's book).
- Talk about how to conclude the argument, summing it up in one or two sentences and stating what the children believe should be done.

Independent work

- Children begin their independent writing.

Plenary

- Review the work in progress, offering help and encouragement.

DAY 4

Big Book 4C p.24 Pupil's Book p.79

Shared reading

- Read 'The Tree House'. How did the children in the poem enjoy the tree? Why was it difficult to build their tree house? How did they solve the problem?
- Ask the children to explain the first verse.
- What do the last two lines of the third stanza mean?
- Ask the children to explain the last two lines of the poem.

Focused word/sentence work

- Investigate suffixes in words from the text, e.g. flowery, favourable, broken, impossible, scrabbling, polished, lowest, branches. Which suffixes make adjectives from nouns or adjectives from verbs? Which is a comparative ending? Which is a plural ending?
- Ask the children to identify the nouns. Use the pluralisation test on them. Which noun cannot be pluralised? (Cattle.) Why not?

Independent work

- Children continue their writing.

Plenary

- Review the children's writing. Are their ideas presented clearly, with points ordered and properly linked together? Have they used facts and figures to support their argument? Does the conclusion sum up their argument? Is their writing convincing?

DAY 5

Big Book 4C p.24; Pupil's Book p.79

Shared reading

- Does the poem rhyme? Although the poem does not have regular rhymes it does have examples of full rhymes, 'ground' and 'around', and partial rhymes, e.g. 'ladder' and 'shoulder', 'wide' and 'by', 'up' and 'rope', 'home' and 'same'.
- Does the poem have a strong rhythm?
- How does the poem make the children feel?
- What pictures does it make in their minds?
- Which lines do they like best? Why?
- How is this poem similar to, and different from, 'In the Wood' by Sheila Simmons (Unit 13).

Focused word/sentence work

- Ask the children to identify words with the letter string *ou*, e.g. favourable, ground, around, shoulders. Discuss how this letter string may have different sounds, e.g. could, route, journey.
- Make lists from words the children suggest, classifying them by pronunciation.

Independent work

- Children explore the letter string *ou* and its different pronunciations.

Plenary

- Review the week's work, consolidating teaching points.

Consolidation and extension

- Encourage the children to present their points of view to the class.
- Hold a class debate on an issue on which there are opposing points of view.
- Design posters to promote the recycling of paper, or an issue the children feel strongly about.

Homework

- Page 26 in the homework book encourages the children to collect words with common endings: *-tion, -sion, -ive, -able, -ible, -our, -ough, -ould.*

Unit 26 Animal Issues

Key Learning Objectives

TL16 To read, compare and evaluate examples of arguments and discussions: letters to press, articles, flyers on animal welfare

TL17 To investigate how arguments are presented, e.g. ordering points to link them together so that one follows from another; how statistics can be used to support arguments

TL18 From examples of persuasive writing, to investigate how style and vocabulary are used to convince the intended reader

TL20 To summarise a sentence or paragraph by identifying the most important elements and rewording them in a limited number of words

TL21 To assemble and sequence points in order to plan the presentation of a point of view

TL22 To use writing frames

TL23 To present a point of view in the form of a letter and a report, linking points persuasively and selecting style and vocabulary appropriate to the reader

TL24 To summarise in writing the key ideas

SL3 To understand how the grammar of a sentence alters when the sentence type is altered

SL4 To use connectives, e.g. adverbs, adverbial phrases, conjunctions, to structure an argument, e.g. *if . . . then; on the other hand . . .; finally; so*

WL7 To collect/classify words with common roots; investigate origins and meanings

Range:	Persuasive writing: flyer, letter
Texts:	Flyer and letter to a newspaper about cruelty to circus animals
Resources:	Big Book 4C pp. 26–29 Pupil's Book 4 pp.80-82 Homework Book 4 p.27: Overworked words: *and, then* Copymaster 25: Words linked by spelling and meaning Copymaster 26: Writing frame for expressing an opinion about pets

DAY 1

Big Book 4C p.26; Pupil's Book pp.80-81

Shared reading

- Discuss what a flyer is. At what audience is this flyer aimed? What is it trying to persuade the reader to do?
- How are its points organised? Which part claims that circus animal suffer cruelty? Which part considers the local issue? Which part explains how the reader can help?
- How does the writer support his argument?
- Ask the children to summarise the writer's points about cruelty to circus animals.

Focused word/sentence work

- Explore changing statements in the flyer into questions and into negatives. Discuss any additions or deletions of words which this involves. Are any changes to punctuation necessary?

Independent work

- Children answer questions on the text.

Plenary

- Review the children's independent text work.

DAY 2

Big Book 4C pp.26-27; Pupil's Book p.81

Shared reading

- Read the letter. What is its purpose and audience? Compare the letter with the flyer. Does it make any claims the flyer does not? Is it likely the writer has read the flyer? What makes you think so?
- What do the children think about this issue? Do they think the arguments are valid? Why? Why do they think the opposite point of view is not put forward? Can they think of any valid reasons to keep circuses with animals?

Focused word/sentence work

- Collect, classify and investigate words from the text with common roots, e.g. press, ex<u>press</u>. Ask what other words the children can think of with this link, e.g. depress, pressure. Challenge the class to find other words with common roots such as *-vent* and *-volve* as in pre<u>vent</u> and in<u>volve</u>.
- Investigate the use of common prefixes: <u>in</u>volve, <u>ex</u>press, <u>pre</u>vent.
- Investigate common suffixes: *-ly, -ty, -ment.*
- Copymaster 25 encourages the children to investigate, collect and classify words with common roots.

Independent work

- Children summarise in writing the key ideas from a paragraph.

Plenary

- Review the children's summaries. Are they concise? How might they be improved?

DAY 3

Big Book 4C pp.26-27; Pupil's Book p.82

Shared writing, including focused word/sentence work

- Discuss the headlines on page 82 in the pupil's book. Ask the children to imagine that these are headlines from the local paper and it is *their* school or homes which the reports are about. How would this affect them? How would it affect their parents, friends, neighbours and other local people?
- Select one headline. Discuss in detail the implications. Make notes.

- Plan a letter to the paper, using the plan in the pupil's book.
- Discuss how to order points, use connectives, and incorporate statistics to organise and strengthen the argument. Consider other ways of adding weight to the protest, e.g. a petition, an opinion poll.
- Who is the intended audience for the letter? Discuss how to suit its style and vocabulary to the reader.

Independent work

- Children begin their independent writing.

Plenary

- Review the work in progress, offering help and encouragement.

DAY 4

Big Book 4C p.28; Pupil's Book p.82

Shared reading

- Introduce the text by asking how many children have pets, and how they look after them.
- What is the issue in the text? In what ways might it be cruel to keep pets? To what extent is the class convinced by this argument?
- Examine how the argument is presented. What is the main idea of each paragraph? How are the points organised? Look for connecting words/phrases, e.g. on the other hand . . ., if . . . then . . ., because, etc.
- How does the writer use statistics to support his argument?
- Discuss the responsibilities of pet owners. Why is it important for a person to think seriously before s/he owns a pet?

Focused word/sentence work

- Experiment with re-ordering sentences. The sentence 'Pet owners can be cruel in more obvious ways' can only be re-ordered to retain meaning by adding words, e.g. 'There are more obvious ways in which pet owners can be cruel'. Some re-orderings destroy meaning, e.g. 'If you look after it well, make sure you own a pet'. Some re-orderings make sense, but change the meaning, e.g. 'Millions of pets keep people'.

Independent work

- Children continue their letters.

Plenary

- Review the children's letters with regard to presentation, its powers of persuasion and appropriate style and vocabulary.

DAY 5

Big Book 4C pp.26-29; Pupil's Book p.82

Shared reading and writing, including focused word/sentence work

- Compare the argument about pets with the one on circus animals. How are the two arguments presented? How are the points organised? Are they balanced arguments or one-sided?
- Encourage the children to choose for themselves one side of the argument: for or against pets. Brainstorm ideas and make lists of points for and against.
- Use the plan in the pupil's book to discuss how to structure the writing.
- Discuss how to order points, use connectives, and incorporate statistics to organise and strengthen the argument.
- Consider the intended reader and the appropriate style and vocabulary.
- Copymaster 26 is a writing frame to help with this activity.

Independent work

- Children present their point of view in writing.

Plenary

Review the children's work. Re-emphasise teaching points.

Consolidation and extension

- Copymaster 25 encourages the children to investigate, collect and classify words with common roots. Discuss with the children the origins and meanings of the words.
- Copymaster 26 is a writing frame for expressing an opinion about pets.
- Ask the children to prepare and read aloud their letters to a newspaper.
- Ask the children to prepare and read aloud their points of view on keeping pets.
- Hold a class debate on keeping pets.

Homework

- Page 27 in the homework book gives practice in avoiding the use of the overworked words *and* and *then*. Discuss with the children ways to do this: by shortening overlong sentences and by using alternative words.

Unit 27 Naledi's Plan

Key Learning Objectives

TL1 To identify social, moral or cultural issues in stories, e.g. the dilemmas faced by characters or the moral of the story, and to discuss how the characters deal with them, to locate evidence in the text

TL2 To read stories from other cultures, by focusing on, e.g. differences in place, time, customs, relationships; to identify and discuss recurring themes where appropriate

TL3 To understand how paragraphs or chapters are used to collect, order and build up ideas

TL8 To write critically about an issue or dilemma raised in the story, explaining the problem, alternative courses of action and evaluating the writer's solution

SL1 To understand that some words can be changed in particular ways and others cannot, e.g. adding comparative endings, pluralisation and that these are important clues for identifying word classes

SL3 To understand how the grammar of a sentence alters when the sentence type is altered

SL4 To use connectives, e.g. adverbs, adverbial phrases, conjunctions, to structure an argument, e.g. if . . . then; on the other hand . . .; finally; so

WL8 To practise extending and compounding words through adding parts; revise and reinforce earlier work (Y3) on prefixes and suffixes

Range:	Short novel that raises an issue; story from another culture
Texts:	Extracts from *Journey to Jo'burg*, Beverley Naidoo
Resources:	Big Book 4C pp.30-34 Pupil's Book 4 pp.83-85 Homework Book 4 p.28: Suffixes: *-ful, -ly, -y, -able, -ive, -ic, -ist*

Preparation

- NB The second text is for shared reading on day 3 in order to provide the necessary background for the writing which, in this unit, is on days 4 and 5.

DAY 1

Big Book 4C pp.30-32; Pupil's Book pp.83-84

Shared reading

- Discuss the background to the story: South Africa in apartheid days. The children's mother has to work and live 300 km away in Johannesburg, leaving them with their granny and aunty.
- What is the issue in this story?
- How does Naledi feel about their situation? Which words and phrases show this?
- What are the key ideas in each paragraph?

Focused word/sentence work

- Investigate the ways paragraphs are introduced and linked, e.g. Each morning . . .; As they came nearer . . .; Finally. . .; It was the school holidays now . . .
- Collect and classify words with common letter strings but different pronunciations, e.g. c<u>oo</u>l (cook), c<u>all</u>ed (sh<u>all</u>), n<u>ow</u> (sn<u>ow</u>); c<u>ou</u>ld and j<u>ou</u>rney.

Independent work

- Children answer questions about the story.

Plenary

- Discuss the children's answers.

DAY 2

Big Book 4C pp.30-32; Pupil's Book p.84

Shared reading

- What does the class think of Naledi's plan? Is it a good idea? What might the consequences be? Can the class suggest an alternative course of action?
- Discuss how life for the children in the story is different from the lives of the children in the class.

Focused word/sentence work

- Experiment with sentence transformations: questions to statements and orders, e.g. 'Can't we take Dineo to hospital?'; affirmatives to negatives, e.g. 'It was the school holidays'; saying the same thing in a different way, e.g. 'Naledi could stand it no longer'; singular to plural and vice versa, e.g. 'Tiro walked down to the village <u>tap</u> with their empty <u>buckets</u>'; past to present tense, e.g. 'Naledi and Tiro were worried'.
- Investigate the differences between certainties and possibilities, e.g.' Dineo might die' and 'Dineo is going to die'.

Independent work

- Children experiment with sentence transformations: singular to plural, present tense to past, affirmative to negative and possibilities to certainties and vice versa.

Plenary

- Review the children's independent work, re-emphasising teaching points and clarifying misconceptions.

DAY 3

Big Book 4C pp.33-34; Pupil's Book p.85

Shared reading

- Day 3 work in this unit focuses on the continuation of the story of Naledi's plan.
- What do the children think about Tiro's objections to Naledi's plan? What might he have said to persuade his sister not to go?
- Do the children think Nono is right in not wanting to frighten Mma? Why?
- Why did Naledi decide not to tell Nono of her plan?
- What do they think Nono will say when she finds they have gone?

Focused word/sentence work

- Ask the children to identify nouns in the text. Which are proper nouns? Sort the common nouns into singular and plural. Which noun does not have a plural? (Money.)
- Ask the children to identify uses of the apostrophe. Which denote contractions and which possession?

Independent work

- Children answer questions about the story.

Plenary

- Discuss the children's answers to the questions.

DAY 4

Big Book 4C pp.33-34; Pupil's Book p.85

Shared reading and writing

- Ask the children to put themselves in Naledi's place. Discuss her problem and her plan. Make a list of its good points and bad points. Can her plan be improved? Would an alternative course of action make more sense?
- Write critically about it in four paragraphs, explaining the problem, outlining the pros and cons of Naledi's plan and suggesting what she do.

Focused word/sentence work

- Discuss the use of connectives to structure the writing, e.g. if, then, on the other hand, so, finally.

Independent work

- Children write about Naledi's plan.

Plenary

- Review the children's work in progress, offering help and encouragement.

DAY 5

Big Book 4C pp.30-34; Pupil's Book p.85

Shared reading

- Read both extracts as a continuous text.
- Identify the opinions of Nono, Tiro and Naledi. Choose children to role play these parts, discussing what should be done.
- Discuss what they could say to Mma in a telegram. Ask the children to explain the situation in as few words as possible.

Focused word/sentence work

- Ask the children to identify the adjectives in the texts. Experiment with adding comparative endings, e.g. big, bigger; scary, more scary. Discuss why we can't do the same with *empty*.
- Experiment with changing questions in the second extract to statements and vice versa.

Independent work

- Children complete their writing.

Plenary

- Discuss the children's evaluation of Naledi's situation.

Consolidation and extension

- Challenge the children with further sentences to transform in a variety of ways.
- Ask the children to prepare a flyer asking people to attend a meeting about building a clinic close to where Naledi lives. Use the flyer in Unit 26 as a model.
- Ask the children to write a letter to Naledi advising her what she should do.

Homework

- Page 28 in the homework book practises adding suffixes: *-ful, -ly, -y, -able, -ive, -ic, -ist.*

Unit 28

A House of Broken Things

Key Learning Objectives

TL1 To identify social, moral or cultural issues in stories, e.g. the dilemmas faced by characters, and to discuss how the characters deal with them, to locate evidence in the text

TL3 To understand how paragraphs or chapters are used to collect, order and build up ideas

TL8 To write critically about an issue or dilemma raised in the story, explaining the problem, alternative courses of action and evaluating the writer's solution

TL13 To write own longer stories in chapters from story plans

SL2 To identify the common punctuation marks including commas, semi-colons, dashes, hyphens, speech marks, and to respond to them appropriately when reading

WL11 To investigate compound words and recognise that they can aid spelling even where pronunciation obscures it, e.g. *handbag, cupboard*

Range:	Short novel that raises an issue
Texts:	Extracts from *The Meteorite Spoon*, Philip Ridley
Resources:	Big Book 4C pp.35-39 Pupil's Book 4 pp.86-89 Homework Book 4 p.29: Compound words

Preparation

- NB The second text is for shared reading on day 3 in order to provide the necessary background for the writing which, in this unit, is on days 3, 4 and 5.
- The longer story in three chapters, which begins on day 4, will need further time outside the literacy hour.

DAY 1

Big Book 4C pp.35-37; Pupil's Book pp.86-87

Shared reading

- What is the issue in this story? How do the children in the class feel when others in the family are arguing? Discuss what life is like for the Thunder children.
- Discuss possible reasons for the constant arguments, e.g. the pressures of unemployment and lack of money. What evidence for this is there in the text?
- In what ways are the Thunders being unfair to their children, e.g. always arguing, making unfavourable references to their appearance? How would the class feel in similar circumstances?
- Consider the plight of the children. What options do Filly and Fergal have to change things? What might the consequences of such actions be?

Focused word/sentence work

- Ask the children to identify the common punctuation marks used in the passage, e.g. commas, speech marks, exclamation marks, dashes, hyphens, brackets, dots. Discuss their functions.
- Ask the children to read the passage aloud. Emphasise the need for intonation appropriate to the grammar and punctuation.

Independent work

- Children answer the questions on the text.

Plenary

- Review the children's independent text work.

DAY 2

Big Book 4C pp.35-37; Pupil's Book p.87

Shared reading

- Ask the children to retell the story.
- Why does the class think the author chose the name Thunder?
- The pupil's book has a continuation extract from *The Meteorite Spoon* as a cloze passage. Investigate how reading beyond the missing word often gives important clues.

Focused word/sentence work

- Ask the children to pick out the verbs for *broken*, e.g. smashed, cracked, shattered. Encourage them to suggest other synonymous verbs and to use them in sentences to show their meaning.

Independent work

Children work on the cloze passage.

Plenary

- Discuss the words selected by the children for the cloze passage. Any word which fits the sense of the passage is acceptable. The actual words used by the author are given here for reference purposes: like, Filly's, face, was, its, the, in, when, only, than, recall, calling, memories, broken, himself, did, time.

DAY 3

Big Book 4C pp.38-39; Pupil's Book p.88

Shared reading and writing, including focused word/sentence work

- Read the second extract from *The Meteorite Spoon*. Discuss Filly's way of cheering up her brother. Do the children think this would work? Ask them to give reasons for their answers.
- What other things might she have done to cheer him up?
- Plan a critical evaluation of the issue in this story, using the suggestions in the pupil's book.

- How effective is Filly's way of coping? What alternative course of action can the children suggest? What might Filly say or do?
- Discuss how connectives will help to structure the children's writing.

Independent work

- Children write critically about the dilemma.

Plenary

- Discuss the children's evaluations of the dilemma of Filly and Fergal.

DAY 4

Big Book 4C pp.38-39; Pupil's Book p.89

Shared reading and writing

- Read the second text again. Discuss what Filly might have written in her book about the three arguments the author refers to. Note that Filly records what each argument is about, how long it lasted and what was broken.
- Tell the children that they are going to write about the three arguments in three chapters, as Filly might have written about them in her book.
- Choose one of the arguments and build a scenario of what happened, using the plan in the pupils book to help you. Make notes for each paragraph.
- Discuss purpose, audience and style. The audience is Filly's seven-year-old brother, Fergal, and its purpose is to cheer him up.

Focused word/sentence work

- Investigate the use of the apostrophe in 'their parents' arguing'. Why does the apostrophe come after the s?
- Investigate the use of capital letters in the titles of books and chapters. Note that only the important words have capitals.
- Remind the children how to set out dialogue.

Independent work

- Children begin the first chapter. This may be continued outside the literacy hour.

Plenary

- Review the children's writing, offering help and encouragement

DAY 5

Big Book 4C pp.35-39; Pupil's Book p.89

Shared reading and writing, including focused word/sentence work

- Ask the children to share their chapters with the rest of the class. Discuss aspects such as style, vocabulary and dialogue.
- Discuss the children's use of punctuation in their dialogue.
- Plan together a second or third chapter.

Independent work

- Children continue writing their chapters, completing them outside the literacy hour.

Plenary

- Review the week's work, consolidating teaching points.

Consolidation and extension

- Publish the children's chapters, with suitable illustrations, as *The Book of Arguments*.
- Those children who are interested might write a further chapter about a different argument.
- Write a shared story of how Filly manages to stop her parents from arguing. Discuss how this would change the reader's view of the characters and events of the original story.

Homework

- Page 29 in the homework book focuses on compound words. Discuss with the children how words such as 'cupboard' and 'handbag' can aid spelling even where the pronunciation obscures it.

Unit 29 Advertisements

Key Learning Objectives

TL18 From examples of persuasive writing, to investigate how style and vocabulary are used to convince the intended reader

TL19 To evaluate advertisements for their impact, appeal and honesty, focusing in particular on how information about the product is presented: exaggerated claims, tactics for grabbing attention, linguistic devices, e.g. puns, jingles, alliteration, invented words

TL25 To design an advertisement, making use of linguistic and other features learnt from reading examples

SL3 To understand how the grammar of a sentence alters when the sentence type is altered

Range:	Persuasive writing: advertisements
Texts:	Crunchy Wheat; The Incredible Robo; slogans and jingles
Resources:	Big Book 4C pp.40-43 Pupil's Book 4 pp.90-92 Homework Book 4 p.30: All change! – changing statements to questions; affirmatives to opposites Copymaster 27: Looking at adverts – evaluation sheet Copymaster 28: Writing an advert – planning sheet

Preparation

- Collect a variety of advertisements for evaluation and comparison. Used in conjunction with copymaster 27 these will provide further practice in evaluating advertisements

DAY 1

Big Book 4C pp.40-41; Pupil's Book pp.90-91

Shared reading

- Discuss the Crunchy Wheat advertisement with the children. What is its slogan? Is this a fact, or something they would like you to believe? What is the main image in the advert? Why do you think they use a 'celebrity' to promote the product? How might this influence sales? Might people be quite so interested if it were Matt Benton, window cleaner, instead of a football star?
- The advertisers make health claims for the cereal. What are these? Which people in the family might be influenced by such claims? How does Matt Benton help this message?
- What does the class think of the Crunchy Wheat Challenge? Is it a real challenge? What is its purpose?
- What does the class think of the special offer? Why does the company make such an offer? What would they gain? What would the consumer have to spend?
- Discuss the Incredible Robo advert. How does it capture attention? Who is it aimed at? How can you tell? Would such a toy appeal to the class? Ask them to give reasons for their answers.

Focused word/sentence work

- Collect and discuss the words and phrases which make each product sound exciting.
- Investigate the effect of these words in a variety of ways. Experiment with deleting them. How does that change the effect? Try substituting synonymous words. How is the meaning affected now?

Independent work

- Children answer the questions about the advertisements.

Plenary

- Review the children's independent text work.

DAY 2

Big Book 4C pp.40-41; Pupil's Book p.91

Shared reading

- Is the claim that Robo is a thinking robot reasonable? Why?
- Which words and phrases make it sound as if the toy is going to sell out fast? Why does the advertiser say these things?
- What important information is left out of the advert? Why do the children think they do not give the price? Why do they want you to send for a catalogue? Do you think £1 is a reasonable price to ask for this? Why?
- Look at the 'Investigating advertisements' section on page 91 in the pupil's book. Select one of the advertisements for evaluation, and discuss answers to the questions.
- The questions are reproduced on copymaster 27. The sheet is suitable for evaluating most advertisements, including television adverts.

Focused word/sentence work

- Experiment with words which make the cereal sound unattractive, e.g. the worst breakfast cereal ever, the boring robot nobody wants, etc.
- Experiment with transforming affirmatives into negatives, e.g. 'Do not collect the special coupons'; '. . . you won't agree', etc. Try making everything its opposite, e.g. 'Every breakfast cereal is healthier'. 'Lots of added sugar'; 'High in fat', etc.
- Experiment with transforming certainties to possibilities, e.g. 'They might be irresistibly crunchy': 'You might agree', etc.

Independent work

- Children evaluate one of the advertisements.

Plenary

- Discuss the children's evaluations of the advertisements, and the greater insight into advertising that the activity has given them.

DAY 3

Big Book 4C pp.40-41; Pupil's Book p.92

Shared reading and writing, including focused word/sentence work

- Tell the children they are going to write an advertisement for a new product. Discuss what that product should be, e.g. a new food or toy.
- Design an advertisement for the product, making notes under the headings given on page 92 in the pupil's book. Copymaster 28 may be used as a planning sheet for this activity.
- Make use of the linguistic features learnt from the Crunchy Wheat and Robo advertisements, or any you have collected.
- Experiment with puns, alliteration and invented words.

Independent work

- Children begin writing their own advertisement.

Plenary

- Review the work in progress, praising examples of good practice, and drawing them to the attention of the rest of the class.

DAY 4

Big Book 4C pp.42-43; Pupil's Book p.92

Shared reading, including focused word/sentence work

- Read the slogans on pages 42-43 in the anthology. Investigate the different ways the advertisers have played with words to produce a memorable jingle, e.g. puns (Drive the Wright way); alliteration (Better Buy a Bostock Bike); rhyme (Creamy Spread – better than butter on your bread); rhythm (Travel Trickett – just the ticket!); invented words (Dentodyne, Dentine X). Note that some jingles use a combination of these devices.
- Discuss each slogan in turn, evaluating its effect. Which do the children think works best? Why? Which is the least successful? Why?
- Discuss slogans from adverts the children know well. What devices are used to make them memorable? How does music contribute to this (in radio and TV advertising)?
- Why is a jingle an excellent way of keeping a product name in the mind?
- Discuss how some jingles can linger in the mind for months, years or even decades, e.g. the 1950's jingle 'You'll wonder where the yellow went when you brush your teeth with Pepsodent'.
- Ask the children to think of a suitable slogan for their advertisements. Encourage them to use one or more of the devices you have identified and discussed.

Independent work

- Children continue work on their advertisements.

Plenary

- Let the children read aloud their completed advertisements. Select suitable examples for later discussion in the shared text part of the lesson on day 5.

DAY 5

Big Book 4C pp.40-43; Pupil's Book p.92

Shared reading

- Read together selected examples of the children's own advertisements.
- Evaluate the advertisements using the questions on page 91 in the pupil's book (see day 2 work).
- Discuss the use of linguistic devices.

Focused word/sentence work

- Ask the children to look for words within words in the jingles in the anthology, e.g. 'mile' in 's<u>mile</u>', 'read' in 'sp<u>read</u>'; 'right' in b<u>right</u>est; 'air' in d<u>air</u>y. Discuss how these can be an aid to spelling.

Independent work

- Children explore words within words.

Plenary

- Review the week's work, consolidating teaching points.

Consolidation and extension

- Copymaster 27 focuses on evaluating adverts. The sheet is suitable for most adverts, including television advertisements.
- Copymaster 28 is a planning sheet for the children's own adverts.
- Display and discuss the children's own adverts. Compare them with the adverts they used as models.
- Encourage the children to invent jingles and compose simple tunes for them.
- Ask the children to adapt their adverts to a radio format, perhaps with music and sound effects. Record them on cassette.

Homework

- Page 30 in the homework book gives practice in transforming statements into questions, and affirmatives into negatives.

Unit 30 A Pattern of Poems

Key Learning Objectives

TL4 To understand the following terms and identify them in poems: verse, chorus, couplet, stanza, rhyme, rhythm, alliteration

TL5 To clap out and count the syllables in each line of regular poetry

TL6 To describe how a poet does or does not use rhyme, e.g. every alternate line, rhyming couplets, no rhyme, other patterns of rhyme

TL7 To recognise some simple forms of poetry and their uses.

TL14 To write poems, experimenting with different styles and structures, discuss if and why different forms are more suitable than others

TL15 To produce polished poetry through revision, e.g. deleting words, adding words, changing words, reorganising words and lines, experimenting with figurative language

SL1 To understand that some words can be changed in particular ways and others cannot: changing verb endings, adding comparative endings, and that these are important clues for identifying word classes

WL7 To collect/classify words with common roots: *phone, press, vent*

Range:	Range of poetry in different forms: haiku, cinquain, couplets, list, thin poems, epitaphs
Texts:	'Black Dot', Libby Houston; 'Quao', Pamela Mordecai; 'Fish', John Cunliffe 'Winter Morning', Ogden Nash; 'Storm', Wes Magee; two epitaphs, Anon; 'Happy Haiku', James Kirkup
Resources:	Big Book 4C pp.44-48 Pupil's Book 4 pp.93-96 Homework Book 4 p.31:Words with common roots: *phone, press, vent* p.32: Revision: *homophones, definitions, changing sentences* Copymaster 29: Self-assessment master Copymaster 30: Revision: assessment master for term 3

DAY 1

Big Book 4C pp.44-47; Pupil's Book pp.93-94

Shared reading

- Read and enjoy the poems.
- Investigate the pattern of the poems. Discuss the different types: thin poem, list, couplets, epitaphs, cinquain. A cinquain is a poem of five lines. Properly, it should have 22 syllables in the sequence 2, 4, 6, 8, 2. 'Storm' is a variation of this format, with lines of different numbers of words: 1, 2, 3, 4,1. This is an easier model for the children to use when writing on days 3 and 4. Encourage the children to clap out the syllables: 1, 4, 4, 4, 1.
- Investigate the use of rhyme. Which poem does not rhyme? Ask the children to identify the rhyming pattern for each of the others, e.g. 'Winter Morning': AA BB CC DD EE (rhyming couplets).

Focused word/sentence work

- Ask the children to identify compound words, e.g. inside, showmen, snowmen, birthday, snowflakes.
- Explore the use of hyphens in 'Black Dot' to make special combinations, e.g. jiggle-tail, belly-flopper.
- Ask the children to find an example of a diminutive prefix: minimal.
- What is the jelly tot in 'Black Dot'? Why are the words effective?

Independent work

- Children answer questions about the poems.

Plenary

- Review the children's independent text work.

DAY 2

Big Book 4C pp.44-47; Pupil's Book pp.93-94

Shared reading

- Look at the pattern of the poems again. How many verses do they have? Are they regular in length? If not, why has the poet written them that way? Why do the lines end where they do?
- Clap out the rhythm of the poems.
- Read each poem in turn. What pictures does each make in the children's mind? How does it make them feel?
- Which poem do the children like best? Why?
- Which do they like least? Why?

Focused word/sentence work

- Ask the children to identify verbs in the poems. Make a list. Which of these are powerful verbs, e.g. lashes, writhe.
- Explore how verbs change when adding endings, e.g. *-s, -ing, -ed.*

Independent work

Children revise verb tense, investigating changing verb endings.

Plenary

Review the children's independent work, re-emphasising teaching points and clarifying misconceptions.

DAY 3

Big Book 4C pp.44-47; Pupil's Book p.95

Shared reading and writing

- Ask the children to read the poems aloud. Which poems sounds best read aloud? Why?
- Ask the children to identify lines or words and phrases which they think are particularly effective.
- Discuss the ideas on page 95 in the pupil's book on using the poems as models for the children's own poems.
- Choose one of these to plan and write together.

Focused word/sentence work

- Discuss the use of puns in the epitaphs.

Independent work

- Children write their own poems.

Plenary

- Review the work in progress. Encourage the children to improve their poems by experimenting with deleting, adding or changing words, and reorganising words and lines.

DAY 4

Big Book 4C p.48; Pupil's Book p.96

Shared reading

- Read and enjoy 'Happy Haiku'.
- Explain that each verse of the poem is written in the Japanese form known as haiku (pronounced hi-koo). Ask the children if they can work out what the structure of a haiku is by counting lines and syllable in each line. A haiku has three lines, with the syllable pattern: 5,7,5. Clap out the syllables.
- Ask the children to say what each verse (haiku) is about. What actions are described? What picture does it make in the children's mind? Which words make the picture clear?
- How does each verse make the children feel?

Focused word/sentence work

- Ask the children to identify the powerful verbs in the poem, e.g. trudging, tumbling.
- Ask the children to identify the adjectives. Experiment with making comparatives.

Independent work

- Children choose a different poem from those on page 93 in the pupil's book as a model for a second poem.

Plenary

* Ask the children to read aloud some of their poems.

DAY 5

Big Book 4C pp.48; Pupil's Book p.96

Shared reading and writing

- Which verse of the poem do the children like best? Why? Might this verse be a poem in its own right?
- It is said that a haiku is just the right length to be spoken in a single breath. Ask the children to test this by reading the poem aloud, one verse each.
- Use the suggestions in the pupil's book to write a shared haiku. If the completed poem does not quite fit the pattern, try deleting, adding or substituting words. Do not worry if you can't find a way to do this: many successful haikus do not meet the strict rules exactly, but are still fine poems.

Focused word/sentence work

- Investigate the use of dashes in the poem. Why has the poet used them? What effect do they have?

Independent work

- Children write their own haiku.

Plenary

- Ask more children to read aloud their poems.
- Review the week's work, consolidating teaching points.

Consolidation and extension

- Encourage the children to revise and improve their poems.
- Make an anthology of the children's poems. Ask the children to design appropriate illustrations. Make a contents page and an index of first lines. Include an 'About the poets' section where each poet writes something about himself and his poem.
- Record the poems on cassette. Design a cassette cover. Sell the cassettes to parents and other interested parties.

Homework

- Page 31 in the homework book focuses on words with common roots: *phone, press* and *vent.*
- Page 32 has revision activities: homophones, writing definitions and changing sentences into the past tense, and changing sentences to give them an opposite meaning.

ASSESSMENT

Copymaster 30 is an assessment master of key word and sentence objectives for term 3, testing the children's ability to construct sentences, distinguish between homophones, change statements into questions and questions into commands, and to use common punctuation marks correctly. Indirectly, it will also test vocabulary, spelling and handwriting. The completed sheet will be useful as a record of progress, together with examples of the pupil's text work.

Copymasters

Name

Fiction book review

Title

Author

Introduction

What is the setting? How does the story begin? How are the characters introduced?

Build up

How does the story build towards the most exciting part?

Main event

What is the main event of the book?

Ending

How does it all end?

Focus on Literacy Teacher's Resource Book 4 © Barry and Anita Scholes, HarperCollins*Publishers* Ltd 1999

Name ______________________

Planning a story

Use this sheet to help you plan a story in four paragraphs. Make notes of your ideas.

Introduction

Set the scene. Introduce your character(s). Begin the action.

____

____

____

Build up

The events which lead up to the main event.

____

____

____

Main event

The most exciting part of the story.

____

____

____

Ending

How it all ends.

____

____

____

____

Draw a picture or diagram to help your planning.

Focus on Literacy Teacher's Resource Book 4 © Barry and Anita Scholes, HarperCollins*Publishers* Ltd 1999

A book thermometer

Take the temperature of a story book with these book thermometers. Cut them out and use them as bookmarks. As you finish each chapter, colour in the temperature graph up to the appropriate mark.

All books have some parts that are more interesting than others and this thermometer will help show you how the author builds up his story into climaxes (the most exciting parts).

Title ____________ **Author** ____________

Chapter	1	2	3	4	5	6	7	8	9	10	11	12	13	14	15	16	17	18	19	20
Impossible to put down																				
Very interesting																				
Interesting																				
Fairly interesting																				
Not very interesting																				

When you have recorded a few books in this way, compare the thermometers. Are the thermometers of books written by the same author similar?

Title ____________ **Author** ____________

Chapter	1	2	3	4	5	6	7	8	9	10	11	12	13	14	15	16	17	18	19	20
Impossible to put down																				
Very interesting																				
Interesting																				
Fairly interesting																				
Not very interesting																				

Focus on Literacy Teacher's Resource Book 4 © Barry and Anita Scholes, HarperCollins*Publishers* Ltd 1999

Copymaster 4
Unit 2

Name ______________________

Finding out about writers

Find out about popular authors and poets. One way to do this is to read about them on the covers of their books. Another is to watch for when they are interviewed on television or are featured in magazines.

A popular author

Name ______________________

Date and place of birth ______________________

Other information ______________________

____

____

____

____

____

First book ______________________

Most popular books ______________________

____

____

My favourite book by this author

____

A popular poet

Name ______________________

Date and place of birth ______________________

Other information ______________________

____

____

____

____

____

First book/poem ______________________

Most popular poems ______________________

____

____

My favourite book/poem by this author

____

Name ______________________

How to . . .

How to write

Planning

- Think about your writing.
- What kind of writing is it?
- Why are you writing it?
- Who are you writing it for?
- Make notes of your ideas.
- Choose your best ideas.
- Make a plan of what you will write.

Drafting and revising

- Write a first draft.
- Read what you have written.
- Have you missed anything out?
- Is everything in the right order?
- Are there any parts which would be better left out, or made more interesting?
- Write a second draft, putting these things right.

Proofreading

- Are there any spelling mistakes? Underline these and check the correct spelling.
- Is the punctuation correct? Circle any errors.

Presenting

- Write a neat, correct and clear final copy.

How to find information

Planning

- What do you want to find out? Write down the key words in your question.
- Where can you find out? Which books, computer software, newspapers, etc. will help you?

Looking for information

- Look for the key words in the index or contents. Write down the page numbers.
- Look for the key words on those pages.
- Make notes of the information you need. Use your notes to answer the questions.

How to learn spellings

Look, Say, Cover, Write, Check

When you have looked up a word in a dictionary, note down its meaning and learn how to spell it.

Look

Say

Cover

Write

Check

Focus on Literacy Teacher's Resource Book 4 © Barry and Anita Scholes, HarperCollins*Publishers* Ltd 1999

Glossary

This glossary lists explanations of specialist words used in studying English. The words in bold in the explanations are also in the main glossary list.

adjective — An adjective describes a **noun**:
a blue bus, a heavy box, interesting books

adverb — An adverb tells us more about a **verb**:
He blows the trumpet loudly. *She drives carefully.*

alliteration — Alliteration is using several words together which begin with the same sound:
Hannah hurried home happily.

alphabet — The letters of the alphabet are:
a b c d e f g h i j k l m n o p q r s t u v w x y z

alphabetical order — Alphabetical order is when words are arranged in the order of the letters of the **alphabet**:
apple, banana, carrot, doughnut.
When words begin with the same letter, look at the second, third or later letters to decide the right order:
bark, belong, belt, busy, butter, button

apostrophe — (') An apostrophe is a raised **comma**. It is used for short forms of words, showing that one or more letters have been missed out:
I'm = I am, don't = do not
It is also used to show that something belongs to someone:
Elizabeth's mother, Carl's coat

author — An author is the writer of a book.

capital letter — A capital letter is used for the first word in a **sentence**, for names of people and places, and the titles of books, newspapers, plays, films, TV programmes, etc:
James, Charlie and the Chocolate Factory, Daily Mail.

question mark — (?) A question mark comes at the end of a question.

rhyme — Words that rhyme sound very similar:
cat, mat; bin, thin; sun, run.

rhythm — Rhythm is a regular beat in poetry or music.

sentence — A sentence is a group of words which make complete sense. A sentence starts with a **capital letter** and ends with a **full stop**, **question mark** or **exclamation mark**.

setting — The setting of a book is where and when the story takes place.

singular — Singular is the form of the word which refers to just one person or thing:
apple, potato, baby, wolf.

speech marks — Spoken words in stories are put inside speech marks:
"What kind of dog is that?" asked David.
Speech marks are also known as inverted commas.

suffix — A suffix is a group of letters which is added to the end of a **root word** to make a new word. Some common prefixes are -ful, -fully, -ness, -less, -able:
hope + ful = hopeful *comfort + able = comfortable.*

synonym — Words with similar meanings are called synonyms. Synonyms can be found in a **thesaurus**:
small, tiny, minute, microscopic, teeny.

tense — Verb tense is the form of the **verb** which tells us when something happens, in the past, present or future:
present tense — *he walks, he is walking*
past tense — *he walked, he was walking*
future tense — *he will walk, he will be walking.*

thesaurus — A thesaurus is a book that has lists of words which have similar meaning. We use a thesaurus to help us choose more interesting words.

verb — A verb is an action word:
He writes. She jumped. They ran. The dog barked.

vowel — The vowels are *a, e, i, o, u*. Sometimes *y* acts as a vowel, e.g. spy.

character	A character is a person in a story.
chapter	A chapter is a section of a book.
comma	(,) A comma is used to separate words in a list: *She wore an old, threadbare, woolly, red coat.* *He took a drink, sandwiches, biscuits and a slice of cake.* A raised comma is known as an **apostrophe.**
consonant	A consonant is any letter which is *not* a **vowel**. The vowels are a, e, i, o, u.
contents	A contents page is a page at the front of a book which tells you what the book contains. It gives **chapter** headings and page numbers.
dialogue	Dialogue in a book, a play or a film is a conversation.
dictionary	A dictionary is a book in which words are listed in **alphabetical order**. It explains the meanings of the words.
definition	A definition explains the meaning of a word.
exclamation	An exclamation is a **sentence** which gives a command, warning or threat. It is also used to show surprise: *Stop!* *What a beautiful picture!* An exclamation ends with an **exclamation mark**.
exclamation mark	(!) An exclamation mark is used at the end of an **exclamation**.
fact	A fact is something which is true.
fiction	Fiction is stories that have been invented by the **author.** The books in a library are usually divided into fiction and **non-fiction** books.
full stop	(.) A full stop comes at the end of a **sentence** that is not a **question** nor an **exclamation**.
glossary	The list you are now reading is a glossary. It is an **alphabetical** list of specialist words and their meanings. It is usually found at the back of a book.
index	An index is an **alphabetical** list of the subjects in a book, together with the pages where they can be found. An index is placed at the back of a book.

non-fiction	Non-fiction is writing that gives facts and information rather than telling a story. The books in a library are usually divided into **fiction** and non-fiction books.
noun	A noun is a naming word. Proper nouns are the special names of people and places: *Louise, Paul, Glasgow, France, Essex.* Nouns that are not proper nouns are common nouns: *book, window, car, rabbit, pencil.* A collective noun names a collection of living things or objects: *a flock of sheep, a class of school children, a string of beads.*
paragraph	A paragraph is a number of **sentences** about the same subject. A new paragraph begins on a new line, and slightly in from the side of the page.
plot	The plot of a book, play, film, etc. is its story.
plural	Plural means more than one: apples , potatoes, babies , wolves.
prefix	A prefix is a group of letters added to the beginning of a word to make a new word. Some common prefixes are un-, mis-, in-, im-, dis-, pre-, re-: *un + tidy = untidy* *dis + approve = disapprove*
pronoun	A pronoun is a word that stands for a **noun**: Jo is clever. *She* is clever. The cat scratched Ian. *It* scratched *him*.
proof reading	Proof reading means checking of a piece of written work carefully.
punctuation	Punctuation refers to marks such as **commas**, **full stops**, **question marks**, **exclamation marks** and **apostrophes**.
question	A question is a **sentence** which asks for information. Questions usually begin with words such as: *Who? Whose? Why? Where? When? How?* A question ends with a **question mark.**

Focus on Literacy Teacher's Resource Book 4 © Barry and Anita Scholes, HarperCollins*Publishers* Ltd 1999

Name

Writing a playscript

Title of the play

Characters

Name | Who they are

Scene

Stage directions

Character's name | **Dialogue**

Name ______

Message in a bottle

Write a message that you might put in a bottle and send out to sea. Tell the person who might find it all about yourself. Say why you are sending it, and what you would like the finder to do when he or she reads your message.

Focus on Literacy Teacher's Resource Book 4 © Barry and Anita Scholes, HarperCollins*Publishers* Ltd 1999

Name ______________________

Rhymes

Find more rhyming words to complete these wordbanks of rhymes.

-ad

bad

glad

-am

jam

lamb

-ee

tree

sea

-in

thin

chin

-ot

blot

trot

-un

stun

bun

Name ____________

Revision

1. Write your own definitions of these words: fork, blackboard, bin.

2. Use each of these words in a sentence of your own to show its meaning.

a) there

b) their

c) too

d) two

3. Think of a suitable adverb for each of these verbs.

a) stop

b) sing

c) leave

d) speak

e) drive

4. Change the above verbs to the past tense and use each one, with its adverb, in a sentence of your own.

Focus on Literacy Teacher's Resource Book 4 © Barry and Anita Scholes, HarperCollins*Publishers* Ltd 1999

Name ______________________________

Name ____________________

Collecting adjectives

Collect adjectives with these suffixes. Write them in the correct wordbank.

-ful	-less
delightful	harmless

-en	-ous
broken	curious

-y	-able
flowery	comfortable

-ing	-ed
dazzling	pleased

Focus on Literacy Teacher's Resource Book 4 © Barry and Anita Scholes, HarperCollins*Publishers* Ltd 1999

Copymaster 14
Unit 14

Name ______________________

Focus on Literacy Teacher's Resource Book 4 © Barry and Anita Scholes, HarperCollins*Publishers* Ltd 1999

Name ______________________

Words which are little used

Many words used in the past are little used today, because fashions and ways of doing things have changed.
Collect such words and write them in these wordbanks.

Transport
omnibus

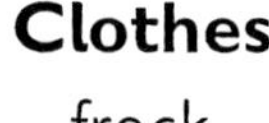

Clothes
frock

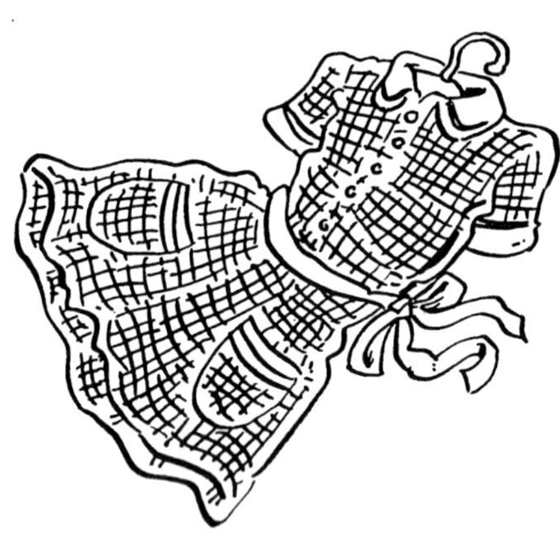

Technology
wireless

Focus on Literacy Teacher's Resource Book 4 © Barry and Anita Scholes, HarperCollins*Publishers* Ltd 1999

Name ____________________

Finding out: planning sheet

When looking for information, use this sheet to help plan your search.

What do I know already? ____________________

What do I want to find out? ____________________

How can I find out? ____________________

Where can I find this information? ____________________

Focus on Literacy Teacher's Resource Book 4 © Barry and Anita Scholes, HarperCollins*Publishers* Ltd 1999

Name ______________________

Copymaster 17
Unit 16

Finding out: finding and recording information

My question:

____

____

____

____

____

____

Write your question here. Underline the key words.

Choose two suitable books from the library.
Write their titles, and your key words below.
Look up your key words in the index. Write the page numbers.

First book title: ______________________________________

1st key word ______________ page numbers ______________

2nd key word ______________ page numbers ______________

3rd key word ______________ page numbers ______________

Second book title: ______________________________________

1st key word ______________ page numbers ______________

2nd key word ______________ page numbers ______________

3rd key word ______________ page numbers ______________

Scan for the information you need. Write the answer to your question:

____

____

____

____

Focus on Literacy Teacher's Resource Book 4 © Barry and Anita Scholes, HarperCollins*Publishers* Ltd 1999

Name ____________________

Focus on Literacy Teacher's Resource Book 4 © Barry and Anita Scholes, HarperCollins*Publishers* Ltd 1999

Name

Copymaster 19
Unit 19

Descriptive writing

Write your own description of one of these. Make a list of suitable words and phrases to use in your description.

Focus on Literacy Teacher's Resource Book 4 © Barry and Anita Scholes, HarperCollins*Publishers* Ltd 1999

Name ____________________

Revision

1. Write your own definitions for these words in as few words as you can.

a) loose ____________ b) mat ____________

c) rich ____________ d) silence ____________

2. Re-order the words in each sentence in two ways: one to keep the same meaning, the other to change it.

a) James took Sally to the library after school.

____

____

____

____

b) He likes bananas, but Kate prefers apples.

____

____

____

____

3. Rewrite these sentences adding adjectives or adjectival phrases to make them more interesting.

a) The man drove the van. ____________

b) The statue stood in a garden. ____________

4. Use each of these words in an interesting sentence of your own: impossible, more, sparkling.

____

____

____

____

Name ______________________

Copymaster 21
Unit 21

Reading record

Keep a record of your reading. Write the titles of the books, comics, magazines and other things you read.

Focus on Literacy Teacher's Resource Book 4 © Barry and Anita Scholes, HarperCollins*Publishers* Ltd 1999

Name ______________________

Comparing books by the same author

Choose two books by the same author you have read and enjoyed. For each book think about the setting, main character, plot (story) and theme (main idea). Write your ideas here.

Author ______________	**Title** ______________	**Title** ______________
Setting Where does the story take place?	**Setting:** ______________ ______________	**Setting:** ______________ ______________
Main character How does he/she behave? What do you think about them?	**Main character:** ______________ ______________ ______________ ______________	**Main character:** ______________ ______________ ______________ ______________
Story What are the main events?	**Story:** ______________ ______________	**Story:** ______________ ______________
Theme What is the main idea of the book?	**Theme:** ______________ ______________	**Theme:** ______________ ______________

In what ways are the two books similar? In what ways are they different?

____

____

____

Which book do you prefer? Why? ______________________

____

____

Focus on Literacy Teacher's Resource Book 4 © Barry and Anita Scholes, HarperCollins*Publishers* Ltd 1999

Name ______________

Book review: a story that raises an issue

Author ______________ **Title** ______________

What problem does the main character face?

What does he/she do about it?

What else might he/she have done?

Focus on Literacy Teacher's Resource Book 4 © Barry and Anita Scholes, HarperCollins*Publishers* Ltd 1999

Name ____________________

Book review: plot

All stories have parts which are more interesting or exciting than others. We call the most exciting part of a story the climax. This is the event which the rest of the story has been building up to.

Author ____________________ **Title** ____________________

What are the events which build up to the climax?

____

____

____

____

____

____

What is the climax of the story?

____

____

____

____

____

____

How does it end?

____

____

____

____

____

____

Focus on Literacy Teacher's Resource Book 4 © Barry and Anita Scholes, HarperCollins*Publishers* Ltd 1999

Name

Words linked by spelling and meaning

Collect words with these common parts.

vent	volve	press
phone	tele	fuse
part	ject	spect
graph	flex	port

Focus on Literacy Teacher's Resource Book 4 © Barry and Anita Scholes, HarperCollins*Publishers* Ltd 1999

Name

Keeping pets

Do you think keeping pets is a good thing, or do you think it is cruel?
Use this sheet to write about it in three paragraphs.

Although some people think ____________________

others believe that ____________________

I think that ____________________

because ____________________

Keeping pets is ____________________

Focus on Literacy Teacher's Resource Book 4 © Barry and Anita Scholes, HarperCollins*Publishers* Ltd 1999

Name

Looking at adverts

What is the advert for? ________________

Who is it aimed at? How can you tell?

How does the advert catch your attention?

What is its slogan? ________________

What pictures does it have? ________________

Write down the words and phrases which make the product seem exciting.

What claims does it make? Are the claims reasonable? Give a reason for your answer.

How else does the advert try to persuade the reader, e.g. competitions, special offers, trial packs, etc? What do you think about them?

What is the most memorable part of the advert? Why?

Focus on Literacy Teacher's Resource Book 4 © Barry and Anita Scholes, HarperCollins*Publishers* Ltd 1999

Name

Writing an advert

Write your own advertisement for a new food, toy, or an item of your choice. Use this planning sheet to help you.

Product name:

Special features:

Market product is aimed at:

Slogan:

Pictures:

Claims about the product:

Promotion, e.g. special offers, competitions, trial packs:

Words and phrases to create interest:

Focus on Literacy Teacher's Resource Book 4 © Barry and Anita Scholes, HarperCollins*Publishers* Ltd 1999

Name ____________________

How am I getting on?

Draw a smiling face ☺ next to the things you enjoy or find easy.
Tick the things you would like more help with. ✔

Speaking, talking and listening

talking about stories or poems

reading aloud by myself

reading aloud with others

Writing

stories

longer stories

playscripts

poems

writing about characters in books

writing about issues in books

letters

reports

instructions

making notes

presenting information

explanations

presenting a point of view

designing advertisements

punctuation

spelling

Reading

story books

poems

plays

newspaper reports

instructions

information books

using a contents page and index

using a dictionary

using a thesaurus

advertisements

other persuasive writing

Focus on Literacy Teacher's Resource Book 4 © Barry and Anita Scholes, HarperCollins*Publishers* Ltd 1999

Name

Revision

1. Use each of these words in a sentence of your own to show its meaning.

a) though ______________________

____

b) through ______________________

____

c) its ______________________

____

d) two ______________________

____

2. Change the statements to questions, and the questions to orders.

a) Will you tidy your room? ______________________

b) You saw what I saw. ______________________

c) Why don't you keep the noise down? ______________________

d) I'm going to Exeter tomorrow. ______________________

e) I could help you with your homework. ______________________

3. Rewrite this passage, putting in all the necessary punctuation marks. Begin a new line for each speaker.

where are you going called neds dad to play out with anu replied ned its tuesday his dad said don't forget were going to grandmas for tea I wont replied ned he set off running in park street

____

____

____

____

Focus on Literacy Teacher's Resource Book 4 © Barry and Anita Scholes, HarperCollins*Publishers* Ltd 1999

Focus on Literacy 4

Achievement Award

Awarded to ______________________________

For ____

Signed ____________________ Date ______________

School ______________________________

Focus on Literacy 4

Achievement Award

Awarded to ______________________________

For ____

Signed ____________________ Date ______________

School ______________________________

Focus on Literacy Teacher's Resource Book 4 © Barry and Anita Scholes, HarperCollins*Publishers* Ltd 1999

RECORD SHEET

NAME ________________ CLASS ________

Year 4 • Term 1

Word level work: phonics, spelling, vocabulary

Objective	Comment
Revision and consolidation from KS1 **1** Reading and spelling words	
Spelling strategies **2** Identifying misspelt words	
3 Spelling strategies	
4 Look, say, cover, write, check	
Spelling conventions and rules **5** Two-syllable words with double consonants	
6 Common homophones	
7 Regular verb endings: *s, ed, ing*	
8 Irregular tense changes	
9 Suffixes: *-al, -ary, -ic, -ship, -hood, -ness, -ment*	
10 Reading and spelling words in Appendix List 2	
Vocabulary extension **11** Defining familiar vocabulary	
12 Alphabetical order to 3rd and 4th place	
13 Using rhyming dictionary	
14 Suffixes: *-ate, -ify*, etc	
Handwriting **15** Using joined handwriting	
16 Matching handwriting to task	
17 Consistency in letter formation, etc	

Sentence level work: grammar and punctuation

Objective	Comment
Grammatical awareness **1** Checking own writing	
2 Tense	
3 Powerful verbs	
4 Adverbs	
Sentence construction and punctuation **5** Commas marking grammatical boundaries	

Text level work: comprehension and composition

Objective	Comment
Fiction and poetry ***Reading comprehension*** **1** Detail building settings and characters	
2 Main characteristics of key characters	
3 Narrative chronology	
4 Narrative order	
5 Playscripts	
6 Charting build-up of playscene	
7 Comparing poems on similar themes	
8 Finding out about popular authors	
Writing composition **9** Different ways of planning stories	
10 Identifying stages in story planning	
12 Linking own experience to historical stories	
13 Writing playscripts	
14 Writing poems	
15 Using paragraphs in story writing	
Non-fiction ***Reading comprehension*** **16** Identifying different types of non-fiction text	
17 Identifying features of non-fiction texts	
18 Examining opening sentences	
19 Understanding the terms 'fact' and 'opinion'	
20 Identifying main features of newspapers	
21 Predicting news stories from headlines	
22 Identifying features of instructional texts	
23 Reading strategies in IT texts	
Writing composition **24** Newspaper style reports	
25 Clear instructions	
26 Using organisational devices	
27 Non-chronological report	

Focus on Literacy Teacher's Resource Book 4 © Barry and Anita Scholes, HarperCollins*Publishers* Ltd 1999

RECORD SHEET

NAME ______________________ CLASS ________

Year 4 • Term 2

Word level work: phonics, spelling, vocabulary

Objective	Comment
Revision and consolidation from KS1 ***Spelling strategies*** **1** Reading and spelling words	
Spelling conventions and rules **2** Identifying misspelt words in own writing	
3 Using independent spelling strategies	
4 Look, say, cover, write, check	
5 Words ending in *f* when suffixes are added	
6 Words with common endings	
7 Prefixes	
8 Read and spell words in Appendix List 2	
Vocabulary extension **9** Alternative words and expressions	
10 Words which imply gender	
11 Vocabulary changes over time	
12 Defining familiar words within varying constraints	
13 Suffixes added to nouns & verbs to make adjectives	
Handwriting **14** Using joined handwriting	
15 Building up speed	
16 Using appropriate style for different purposes	
17 Consistency in size and proportion of letters	

Sentence level work: grammar and punctuation

Objective	Comment
Grammatical awareness **1** Adjectives: – constructing adjectival phrases – comparative and superlative adjectives – comparing adjectives on a scale of intensity – suffixes indicating degrees of intensity – using with adverbs indicating degrees of intensity	
Sentence construction and punctuation **2** Apostrophe to mark posssession	
3 Significance of word order	
4 Commas, connectives and full stops to join and separate clauses	

Focus on Literacy Teacher's Resource Book 4 © Barry and Anita Scholes, HarperCollins*Publishers* Ltd 1999

Text level work: comprehension and composition

Objective	Comment
Fiction and poetry ***Reading comprehension*** **1** How writers create imaginary worlds	
2 How settings influence events and affect behaviour	
3 Comparing settings across a range of stories	
4 How expressive language creates moods, arouses expectations, builds tension, describes attitudes or emotions	
5 Figurative language in poetry and prose	
6 Identifying clues which suggest poems are older	
7 Identifying different patterns of rhyme and verse	
8 Reviewing a range of stories	
9 Recognising texts targeted at particular readers	
Writing composition **10** Developing use of settings in own writing	
11 Writing poetry-based models	
12 Collaborating to write stories in chapters	
13 Writing descriptive, expressive language	
14 Notemaking	
Non-fiction ***Reading comprehension*** **15** Appraising non-fiction books for content and usefulness	
16 Preparing for factual research	
17 Scanning for key words, etc; using to summarise text	
18 Marking extracts by annotating and by selecting key headings, etc	
19 Understanding how and why paragraphs are used to organise information	
20 Key features of explanatory texts	
Writing composition **21** Making short notes	
22 Filling out brief notes into connected prose	
23 Collecting and presenting information from variety of sources	
24 Using paragraphing, link phrases and organisational devices	
25 Explaining a process	

Focus on Literacy Teacher's Resource Book 4 © Barry and Anita Scholes, HarperCollins*Publishers* Ltd 1999

RECORD SHEET

NAME ______________________ CLASS ________

Year 4 • Term 3

Word level work: phonics, spelling, vocabulary

Objective	Comment
Revision and consolidation from KS1 **1** Reading and spelling words	
Spelling strategies **2** Identifying misspelt words in own writing	
3 Using independent spelling strategies	
4 Look, say, cover, write, check	
Spelling conventions and rules **5** Exploring letters and letter strings	
6 Common letter strings with different pronunciations	
7 Words with common roots	
8 Extending and compounding words through adding parts	
9 Suffixes *-ible, -able, -ive, -tion, -sion*	
10 Apostrophe: possessive and contractions	
Vocabulary extension **11** Compound words	
12 Diminutives	
Handwriting **13** Using joined handwriting	
14 Building up speed	
15 Using a range of presentational skills	

Sentence level work: grammar and punctuation

Objective	Comment
Grammatical awareness **1** Changing verb, adjective and noun endings	
Sentence construction and punctuation **2** Identifying common punctuation marks	
3 Changing sentence types	
4 Using connectives	

Text level work: comprehension and composition

Objective	Comment
Fiction and poetry ***Reading comprehension*** **1** Identifying social, moral or cultural issues in stories	
2 Reading stories from other cultures	
3 How paragraphs and chapters collect, order and build-up ideas	
4 Understanding the terms: 'verse', 'chorus', 'couplet', 'stanza', 'rhyme', 'rhythm', 'alliteration'	
5 Clapping out and counting syllables in regular poetry	
6 Describing how a poet does or does not use rhyme	
7 Recognising some simple forms of poetry and their uses	
8 Writing critically about an issue	
9 Reading further stories or poems by a favourite writer	
10 Describing and reviewing own reading habits	
Writing composition **11** Writing own story about a dilemma	
12 Writing alternative ending for known story	
13 Writing own longer stories in chapters from story plans	
14 Writing poems with different styles and structures	
15 Producing polished poetry through revision	
Non-fiction ***Reading comprehension*** **16** Reading, comparing and evaluating arguments and discussions	
17 Investigating how arguments are presented	
18 Investigating style and vocabulary in persuasive writing	
19 Evaluating advertisements	
20 Summarising a sentence or paragraph	
Writing composition **21** Planning presentation of a point of view	
22 Using writing frames	
23 Present a point of view in writing	
24 Summarising key ideas in writing	
25 Designing an advertisement	

Focus on Literacy Teacher's Resource Book 4 © Barry and Anita Scholes, HarperCollins*Publishers* Ltd 1999

Appendices

Focus on Literacy and the NLS Objectives

Term 1

Word level	Sentence level	Text level
1 Continuous work	**1** Unit 3,5,8	**1** Unit 1,2,3,4
2 Continuous work	**2** Unit 1,3,4,5,9,10	**2** Unit 1,2,3
3 Continuous work	**3** Unit 1,3,5,6,7,10	**3** Unit 1,2,3
4 Continuous work	**4** Unit 2,4,6,7,8,9,10	**4** Unit 1,3
5 Unit 4	**5** Unit 2,3,4,7,8	**5** Unit 7
6 Unit 1,2,7,8		**6** Unit 7
7 Unit 1,2,3		**7** Unit 6,10
8 Unit 3,9,10		**8** Unit 2
9 Unit 2,4		**9** Unit 1,3
10 Continuous work		**10** Unit 1,3,4
11 Unit 4,6,8,10		**11** Unit 2
12 Unit 5,8		**12** Unit 3,4
13 Unit 6,10		**13** Unit 7
14 Unit 5		**14** Unit 6,10
15 Continuous work		**15** Unit 1,3,4
16 Continuous work		**16** Unit 4,5,8,9
17 Continuous work		**17** Unit 4,5,8,9
		18 Unit 5,8,9
		19 Unit 8,9
		20 Unit 8,9
		21 Unit 8,9
		22 Unit 5
		23 Unit 8
		24 Unit 8,9
		25 Unit 5
		26 Unit 5
		27 Unit 9

Term 2

Word level	Sentence level	Text level
1 Continuous work	**1** Unit 11,12,13,14,18,20	**1** Unit 11,12,14,15,20
2 Continuous work	**2** Unit 19,20	**2** Unit 11,12,14,15,20
3 Continuous work	**3** Unit 11,13,15,16,17,20	**3** Unit 12,14,15,20
4 Unit 11	**4** Unit 13,16,20	**4** Unit 11,12,13,14,15,20
5 Unit 16		**5** Unit 11,12,13,14,19,20
6 Unit 18		**6** Unit 18,19
7 Unit 14		**7** Unit 13,19
8 Unit 11		**8** Unit 14,15
9 Unit 12,15		**9** Unit 14
10 Unit 16,19		**10** Unit 11,12,14,20
11 Unit 15,19		**11** Unit 13,19
12 Unit 11,13,14,15,17,18,20		**12** Unit 15
13 Unit 13		**13** Unit 11,12,14,15,19,20
14 Continuous work		**14** Unit 16,17,18
15 Continuous work		**15** Unit 16
16 Continuous work		**16** Unit 16
17 Continuous work		**17** Unit 16,17,18
		18 Unit 16,17,18
		19 Unit 16,17,18
		20 Unit 16,17,18
		21 Unit 16,17,18
		22 Unit 16,17,18
		23 Unit 16
		24 Unit 16,17,18
		25 Unit 16,17,18

Term 3

Word level	Sentence level	Text level
1 Continuous work	**1** Unit 22,23,27,30	**1** Unit 21,22,23,27,28
2 Continuous work	**2** Unit 24,28	**2** Unit 21,27
3 Continuous work	**3** Unit 21,22,25,26,27,29	**3** Unit 21,22,27,28
4 Continuous work	**4** Unit 21,25,26,27	**4** Unit 23,24,30
5 Unit 21,22		**5** Unit 24,30
6 Unit 21,24,25		**6** Unit 24,30
7 Unit 26,30		**7** Unit 24,27,30
8 Unit 23,27		**8** Unit 21,22,23,28
9 Unit 23,25		**9** Unit 22,23,24
10 Unit 22		**10** Unit 21
11 Unit 28		**11** Unit 21,23
12 Unit 24		**12** Unit 23,28
13 Continuous work		**13** Unit 28
14 Continuous work		**14** Unit 24,30
15 Continuous work		**15** Unit 24,30
		16 Unit 25,26
		17 Unit 25,26
		18 Unit 25,26,29
		19 Unit 29
		20 Unit 25
		21 Unit 25,26
		22 Unit 26
		23 Unit 25,26
		24 Units 25,26
		25 Unit 29

High and medium frequency words to be taught through Year 4

Term 1

ask(ed)
began
being
brought
can't
change
coming
didn't
does
don't
found
goes
gone
heard
I'm
jumped
knew
know
leave
might
opened
show
started
stopped
think
thought
told
tries
turn (ed)
used
walk (ed) (ing)
watch
write
woke (n)

Term 2

almost
always
any
before
better
during
every
first
half
morning
much
never
number
often
only
second
sometimes
still
suddenly
today
until
upon
while
year
young

Term 3

above
across
along
also
around
below
between
both
different
following
high
inside
near
other
outside
place
right
round
such
through
together
under
where
without